Go-getter

Raise your mojo,
shift your mindset
and thrive

Emma **McQueen**

The perfect book for female leaders
and entrepreneurs

Contents

Gratitudes

Every night at dinner, my family and I talk about what we are grateful for that day. Every Friday, within the Thriving Women community, we tell each other what we are grateful for.

Being grateful is something I aspire to be. Yes, there are moments when I am grateful, but I still have a long way to go. This book would not have been possible without an array of individuals:

Thank you to the hubster, Mark, for kicking ideas around with me and allowing me the space to get this book done.

To my three gorgeous daughters, Olivia, Lily and Evie. May you grow up to be go-getters and know that anything is possible if you put your mind to it. And may you grow up to be kind and generous of spirit. Thank you also for all the laughs, words of encouragement, offers of cups of tea and reminding me not to take myself so seriously.

Jessica Randall and Serena Francis – Team Emma McQueen does not run on its own. Thank you to Jess and Serry, who are the powerhouse behind Emma McQueen. They listen to my crazy ideas, work things into the calendar that only a calendar ninja could, and are a step ahead of me as we roll out new programs. I could not do what I do without you two, you know I think you are both amazeballs, but now it's in writing!

I would also like to thank my amazing colleagues and mentors who have become solid advocates and friends along the way. They helped me believe a book was possible and encouraged me to get my thoughts out there. I feel privileged to do the work I do in my business every day and for this I am extremely grateful. Dr Richard Hodge, Mary Butler, Callum McKirdy, Alex Hagan, Chris Ashmore, Paul Matthews, Alicia McKay, Cam Fink, Jane Anderson and Belinda Brosnan, thank you for all the encouragement and allowing me to freak out a little as I went through this process.

To my circle of Thriving Women. When I created the Thriving Women program, I had a hunch, but what it turned into, well, it was magic! When you go out on a limb and create something you think is going to work and then you get just as much out of it as the group does, you know you are onto a winner. Special mention must go to Holly Cardamone for being my cheerleader, my unofficial/official Communications Director and a genuinely awesome person who is not only a client but a true friend. I feel blessed that I knew you were my people and you agreed! Without you, I would certainly not have had as many words on these pages and I am grateful for your encouragement along the way.

Introduction

I searched high and low for a book written especially for women leaders. I know how that sounds, and I know I could potentially be upsetting a whole population group. But I am okay with that.

This book is written by a woman for women. I wrote this book because there is a lot we think about, wrestle with, work with and juggle that we either don't speak about because we "should" be able to hold it together, or because we don't want to ask for help.

Through the pages of this book, I hope you will see there is a different way to get what you need and want. You *can* have more, and I fully embrace the idea that we can have it all – just not necessarily all at the same time.

I have never been one to sit on the fence. However, in a previous life, I did not use my voice as well as I could have. So, this book is my way of letting my voice be heard. I hope that by reading it and hearing stories from real women, real women like you and me, you will feel less alone. Above all, I hope you will be inspired and know it's never too late to make a change.

The Facts: Barriers We Face

I work with all types of women. Women who are starting their own businesses or stepping into leadership roles. These women are talented, smart and have great potential, yet they are not being paid what they're worth, they are struggling with overwhelm and inaction, and they don't know how to change.

This is compounded by the barriers we must contend with daily. Let's look at some stark facts:

Women are growing businesses: In the past decade, we've seen a significant increase in female owner-operated activity. This is a trend that does not seem to be slowing. In January 2019, there were 715,300 women business operators in Australia (or 34.9% share of all business operators), compared with 1.3 million (65.1%) men business operators. This was an increase of 46,600 (or 2.0%) over the past 12 months. Furthermore, women who operated their own business made up 12.1% of the 5.9 million employed Australian women. Men who operated their own business represented 19.8% of the 6.7 million employed Australian men.[1]

Women are leaving the workforce to pursue meaningful employment on their terms. Many of these businesses start as (or are still) a "side hustle", meaning women are working longer, harder and more intentionally than ever before. According to the Australian Bureau of Statistics (ABS), 15% of females are working more than 58 hours per week.

Women are growing in leadership roles: Many women are also staying in the workforce. While some would say progress could be accelerated, according to the ABS, in the past decade, there has been a growth of women in senior leadership roles from 21% to 38%. However, while the percentage of women in leadership roles has increased, pay equity still requires work, with the gender pay gap sitting at around 15%.[2]

Women still do more of the housework: Many women in business and leadership roles are dealing with "the juggle". Thirty-three per cent of female business owners juggle business and leadership with children under 15 years of age and 4% are the sole carer of those children. In fact, on average, women spend 64% of their working week performing unpaid care work. They spend almost twice as many hours performing such work each week compared to men. The rise of the term "mental load" took hold in 2018–2019, with women reporting carrying the psychological burden of home duties on top of the physical pressure of work, leadership or running of a business.

Women are not looking after themselves as they should: With the juggle of work and family life, the first casualty is usually the care we need for ourselves. We give so much of our time, energy and attention to others, we forget our needs.

Women struggle with confidence: There is much written on confidence, what it is, how to get it, how to build it. Women are tough on themselves; they push themselves to be the best they can be and when they fall short, they judge themselves and rehash it in their minds over and over, making it difficult to let go and get on with it. It seems to take us a bit longer to forgive ourselves and reset.[3]

Women tend to be perfectionists: I am not a perfectionist; I never have been. I was always a 80/20 (probably more like a 50/50, actually!). This attitude did not help me academically, but it has helped me in business. I will make decisions with the information at hand and largely don't stress about making them. After speaking with women about confidence and the link to perfectionism, it occurred to me that we over-prepare, revise and rehearse to ensure we know all the facts, inside out, to feel confident about our decisions. Lynne Cazaly recognises this tendency in her book, *Ish : The Problem with Our Pursuit for Perfection and the Life-Changing Practice of Good Enough,* which helps us to look at our lives and ask ourselves, "Is good enough actually good enough?" I love this premise, because I think if we were all a little more "ish", we would stress less and be happier. #justsaying

So, what gets in the way? Too often, it's the stories we create in our heads.

In my work as a business coach, I have found that our ability to overcome these barriers relates to the following three elements:

1. Mindset

The *Oxford Dictionary* defines "mindset" as "the established set of attitudes held by someone."

The mind is strong, yet it is also like a sponge. If you feed it good, positive stuff, then chances are, this will convert into positive actions. Likewise, if you feed it crap, you will see the unhealthy nature of this as well. What are you feeding your mind? How does this translate into results?

Dr Carol Dweck, author of *Mindset: The New Psychology of Success*, coined the phrase "growth mindset" in 1988. Actually, she coined two phrases: "fixed mindset" and "growth mindset". People with a fixed mindset believe their intelligence is a fixed trait and cannot be changed or developed. They also believe that "natural" talent leads to success, and effort is not required.[4]

On the other hand, people with a growth mindset believe their learning and intelligence can be developed with time and experience. They don't see intelligence as a fixed trait; rather, if they put in the right sort of effort and practise, it can grow.[5]

Dweck says that because people with a growth mindset know their intelligence can be developed, this leads to a desire to learn. They are more likely to embrace challenges, persist when the going gets tough, see effort as the path to mastery, learn from feedback and, as a result, reach higher levels of achievement.[6]

What kind of mindset do you think you have? Is it more fixed or growth? How does this affect your ability to get results?

I talk about results a lot. A LOT.

The very being of me wants to achieve. To me, achievement is like breathing. If I am not achieving and striving for something, I admit, I feel a little lost.

The funny thing is, I'm not that competitive with others. In fact, I am probably more ambivalent than anything else when it comes to my peers. But I still like to achieve in whatever I am doing, and I want to learn and grow and be better than I was yesterday. I attract clients like that, too. You have probably heard the saying "your vibe attracts your tribe," and, in my experience, this is oh so true.

Here's the thing, though: you can't get the results you want if you don't have the mindset to get you there. Many of the clients I work with know that if they want results, they need to undergo a mindset shift. In the words of Henry Ford, "If you always do what you've always done, you'll always get what you've always got."

So, working on our mindset is a task we must do carefully. We must work out the barriers we need to break through, the thoughts we need to challenge (hello, inner critic!) and the patterns we need to change.

2. Mojo

The *Oxford Dictionary* defines "mojo" as "influence, especially magic power."

I love the word mojo – the way it rolls off the tongue, the way it's vague enough to encompass so many things but strong enough that people know what you're talking about.

Mojo is about energy. It's having the energy to get you through the day, the week, the trying times of small kiddies, the times when your kids become teens and think you have no idea, the times when it's tough at work, when you think you can't possibly take on one more thing or make another decision. Managing our mojo means putting ourselves first – something we women are not very good at. You've no doubt heard the overused expression "you can't pour from an empty cup." Well, it's true. Unless we take care of ourselves, no one else will do it for us. Seriously, the time is now.

Mojo is also about kindness and generosity. I talk a lot about these two things because I value them. I also talk about them because we do not give ourselves enough. We are kind and generous to our colleagues and friends when they have an issue; we sit with a listening ear and an open heart. But do we do that for ourselves? Do we cut ourselves some slack or do we beat up on ourselves time and again?

3. Motivation

The *Oxford Dictionary* defines "motivation" as "a reason or reasons for acting or behaving in a particular way."

Motivation is a funny thing. It can lead us in the right direction, the wrong direction or simply put us in a spin. We can second-guess ourselves, wonder if we are doing the right thing, stress whether the timing is right, then beat ourselves up about the decisions we make over and over again.

But when we get our mindset, mojo and motivation right, we begin to change. We become enthusiastic, optimistic and energetic. We start breaking down barriers, working towards unlocking our potential, doing work we love, getting the results we desire, and we thrive. We become go-getters!

This book will show you how. In these pages, we will delve further into the issues women face, as well as the three elements of success. Then, we will explore the 12 most tightly held myths that hold women back from reaching their full potential. Importantly, we will bust these myths and discover what accelerates women's performance, potential and profits, using real-life client examples of these myths and truths at work (all names have been changed to protect people's privacy).

Let's begin!

The Conversations We Have With Ourselves

A conversation was happening. One woman was recounting her day to another.

That morning, the woman had locked herself out of the house. She had to climb through the doggy door to get back in. Once inside, she got herself together and headed to work. She was running late by this stage. She grabbed a coffee on her way to work, but as she got out of her car, she spilled her coffee all over her crisp, white top. She wondered if she should turn around and go back to bed.

She pushed on. She had a deadline to meet, and she needed to nudge some of her co-workers to hit her deadline. But she couldn't get her technology to work. She logged on and off five times and had to take it to the technology department to get it sorted. By the time she got her computer back, she had missed her deadline. She did manage to get the job done and get her work in, but it was two hours after deadline. Her boss gave her some constructive feedback about her lack of planning. Yeah, it had been a tough day.

Upon hearing this, the other woman looked at her thoughtfully and said, "Suck it up, princess. We all have bad days. How on earth did you manage to lock yourself out of your house, and how did you even fit through the doggy door to get back inside? You really need to get in better shape. You should have skipped the coffee – look what happened there. You should have gone back to bed; you obviously weren't prepared for the day ahead. That technology thing, that wasn't your computer, that was your stupidity. Of course you missed your deadline because you're a dimwit. I'm surprised you didn't get fired today, yet you live to tell the story. Keep faking it until you make it, okay?"

Being a woman leader within an organisation or an owner of a business is hard, unappreciated work. We work as hard as the next person, if not a little harder, because we have to break through all those stereotypical barriers. We hope our work speaks for itself, yet deep down, we know it doesn't. The woman in the story is resilient, adaptable and determined, and despite all the things she endured that day, she came through the other side. She is me; she is you; she is all of us at some point or another.

One of the things that gets in our way is that pesky inner voice. You know the one – it sits on your shoulder and tells you that you can't, that you're not good enough. You wonder if you can pull this off, if you will fail. Actually, you wonder *when* you will fail, not if. You wonder when people will find out that you know absolutely nothing. You wonder if you have the energy to keep going, how you will meet everyone's expectations and needs and have some time for yourself.

The story I told is a classic example of how we talk to ourselves, that annoying inner critic who never lets up. We would not talk to each other like that (and if you do have a friend like this, please fire them), so why do we talk to ourselves this way?

A State Of Paralysis

I find what happens is we get thrown so much stuff, we end up with a lot of chatter and clutter in our head, which gives us that overwhelmed feeling. Do you know what I am talking about? We don't know how we got here, and we are not sure how to move forward. We get paralysed at the thought of taking the next step.

Your brain feels foggy because you are juggling all those balls. And they feel like glass balls – you can't drop any of them. It's like driving a car on a winter's day, and the windscreen keeps fogging up until the car has heated up enough to keep the fog away. How good does it feel when you finally keep the fog at bay, and you can see clearly? That's what we all want – that clarity.

When we have clarity and can see exactly where we are going and map our goals, making small steps towards those goals each day, we get a renewed sense of confidence. It pushes us forward. It quietens that inner critic, and we learn to manage that negative voice in our head. We start to question that voice and pop it back in its place. We move beyond paralysis and push forward until we get results, then we see more results. How good does it feel when we get those results?! It's like getting to the top of a steep mountain.

The results will look different for you and for me. Results might be an increase in the bottom line, it might be keeping the lights on for another few months, it could be getting results through your people, keeping your top talent, nailing that project you have been sweating over, it could be increasing sales, it might be getting one client on board. Or it could be getting through the day.

We all want to kick goals, whether it be in our job, inside an organisation, running our own business, sitting on a board or in our community. At some point or another, we all want to see results. Isn't this why we go to the gym, exercise and practise mindfulness? We want to see a result. It might be to look good, feel good, or to dull that negative voice in our head.

My fundamental belief is that everyone should use their passion to propel them forward. We need to tap into our potential and understand our purpose for why we do what we do. There are so many people out there who hate their jobs and don't feel fulfilled in their roles – it's truly a waste. According to Gallup, a whopping 85% of people worldwide hate their jobs![7] Surely, life is too short to perform a job you hate.

As women, we forget to value ourselves. I work with so many women who do not value themselves enough, and they certainly don't get paid their worth. Recently, one of my clients secured a great role, which was a genuine step up for her, *and* she got a $50,000 pay increase and a substantial budget for professional development. I joked with her that finally she was getting paid what she deserved.

Chaos And Confusion

Being stuck in chaos sucks. There are so many of us who feel stuck in the overwhelm of life, unable to figure out what to do next. Being stuck brings out the worst in us. It hurts our family and our relationships. It feels like you're in a traffic jam, with no control and no way out.

But we can use this as an advantage – a personal tipping point, if you like – to do something differently.

I met Jane through a mutual colleague. She came to me because she felt stuck. She was in chaos. She had two roles within major corporate organisations and what she described as a "side hustle", which was a small business, but she was not happy. She had set up this structure to accommodate her family's needs at the time. And, over time, as her kids grew older and she had been with each organisation for longer, the scope of her work had shifted so much that she had zero time for herself.

She was overwhelmed and overworked, on the cusp of throwing it all in, as she couldn't figure out what to do next.

What I suggested floored her (and, I have to say, a few cuss words were sent in my direction!). I asked her to do nothing.

Jane was confused. "That is ridiculous, Emma. I can't do nothing!" Hence, a rather heated debate ensued. It was good – she got it all out, we kicked around some solutions, and she knew something had to change because of the pain she found herself in. I asked her to do nothing because, well, when was the last time you did nothing, and I mean NOTHING? You probably can't even remember. The issue is that when we continue to be busy, no answers come to us, just more problems.

So, Jane agreed to try to do nothing for a short period of time each day. But we didn't stop there. I am unable to sit opposite someone who is in pain and not help them, so we got to work. We looked at all the options, we prioritised, we stopped and let go of what we could, and we made some decisions. It was a big session, and I could see Jane was exhausted but utterly happy with the outcome.

You need to be confused sometimes. Confusion can see us behave in two main ways: we go into panic mode, which sets off those around us, like domino pieces; or we act like a turtle and go into our shell.

Confusion feels like you have a foggy brain that you cannot clear. It comes with a sense of paralysis – you don't know what you need to do next, so it's easier to do nothing (although not in Jane's case, apparently!). I don't mean the forced nothing; I mean the "I do not know what to do next, so my brain is going to shut down" paralysis. But confusion can also be the beginning of significant change.

It's critical we move beyond paralysis. Sometimes, anything is better than nothing (and, yes, I realise I have just contradicted myself, but bear with me). You've got to get the activity going, the immediate next step. For Jane, we forced her into confusion, but we had an action plan that helped her take the immediate next steps with some decisions attached to them (and then she was allowed to do nothing – see what I did there?). In other words, Jane got clarity.

Clarity And Confidence

Clarity is easier said than done, isn't it? Clarity is so important for ourselves, our employees and our suppliers. They all need clarity to deliver what is necessary, to focus on the right things to ensure the results are achieved. We move out of confusion into clarity, and we breathe a sigh of relief, but not before we have done some solid thinking about a clear path forward. Clarity is asking yourself a tonne of questions to get crystal-clear thinking.

I was working with a group of executives, who told me their staff were unable to get results. I dug a little deeper, popped my listening ears on and found out that not all the executives felt this way, but at least half of them did.

When I started doing some investigation in the organisation, it became apparent that those not delivering had no clarity or idea of what they needed to do. Now, if this issue was with one group, it would have been easier to manage, but it involved several groups. The groups that were delivering had clear vision and purpose, and they knew how they were going to get there.

So, can clarity affect a large organisation? Of course it can! Can it make corporates go broke? You betcha!

Clarity gives you the confidence to step into your awesomeness. When you feel confident, your demeanour shifts, you trust your gut more, you stop second-guessing yourself, and people want what you have.

As the *Daily Maverick* says, "Confidence is like compound interest: in the short term it's hard to notice, in the long term, it's crucial."[8]

Confidence gets belief. Remember when you did something new? Learnt a new language or how to play a new sport? Were you good at it straight away? Or were there times when, if you were learning a new language, instead of saying, "Hello, my name is Emma, how are you?" you said, "Would you like some soup with those eggs?" Learning something new takes time. When you learn a new language, you have to learn the basics first, and, once you master the basics, you learn the more complicated variations. When you get it wrong, you repeat and ensure you get it right, then you feel confident to move on, right? So, we have little wins along the way. We gain momentum and we think, "Yes, I'm doing this." Bit by bit, we believe that we can do this.

Conviction And Engagement

Marie got a promotion. Boy, was she ready. After investing heavily in her professional and personal development, she was prepared to lead a much larger team. Her new team was excited about her taking over, and her confidence was contagious. She was optimistic about the future and grateful for the opportunity.

What set Marie apart was her conviction. When you have unwavering conviction in yourself, you inspire others. We all have had leaders who have inspired us, whom we revered because they oozed "solidness". We are drawn to these people. You have seen it, but not only that, you may have felt this solidness yourself. You reach a point when you are sure you have what it takes. Living in conviction is like being solid as a rock. You are stable, tethered to the ground. I had the pleasure of working with such a leader recently, a CEO who had a quiet confidence about her. She was calm, optimistic and knew her-stuff. She was humble and kind but had conviction in herself. She was self-assured. Her people loved her.

As you move through chaos to confusion, finding clarity and confidence, then finally leading with conviction, not only do you start to enjoy your work more, you realise that others around you are engaged, and it feels *oh so good*.

I want to tell you about Becky. Becky worked super hard on herself. She realised that firstly, she needed to be clear to lead her department. She also knew she needed to articulate that clarity and make sense of it for others in a way that inspired them to take action. Because Becky was full of confidence and conviction, she was able to inspire her team to achieve more. You see, when you enjoy your work, you feel a sense of accomplishment. Your team also enjoys their work and everyone feels "in flow", like that's exactly where they should be.

When you feel engaged, you also become more effective in what you are doing. Effectiveness means focusing on the right things, in the right order, at the right time.

Robert Half released a study about the 12 characteristics of being an effective manager.[9] The list looks something like this:

1. An effective manager understands the value of employees.
2. They express gratitude (my personal favourite).
3. They communicate clearly.
4. They listen effectively (did you know that 55% of our day is spent listening, yet only 2% of us have been trained how to listen?[10]).
5. They make decisions.
6. They trust their employees to achieve.
7. They resolve conflicts.
8. They get to know their employees.
9. They set a good example.
10. They are transparent.
11. They are high achievers.
12. They stay a step ahead.

In summary, being effective means you have what it takes to "just get it done". This is made up of a lot of pieces, isn't it?

Take Audrey, for example. She works for a professional services firm and manages a large customer-facing team. She is highly engaged in her role and is excellent at it, and she has highly engaged staff in what can be a challenging role for some of them. She ensures their wellbeing is at the forefront of everything she does. She is compassionate while also keeping an eye on the results because she knows happy employees mean happy customers.

The term "employee experience" gets bandied about a lot these days. Having come from an employee experience background, I know first-hand how difficult it is to ensure employees have a great working experience with your organisation. I love Richard Branson's famous quote, "Clients do not come first. Employees come first. If you take care of your employees, they will take care of the clients." If you are committed to your employees having a great experience with you, your clients will also have a great experience. When you sit in conviction, you inspire your people and push them to be a better version of themselves rather than merely turning up to work. You can give them a sensational employee experience.

Imagine working in an organisation where the employee experience was just as important as the customer experience. Wouldn't that be awesome?

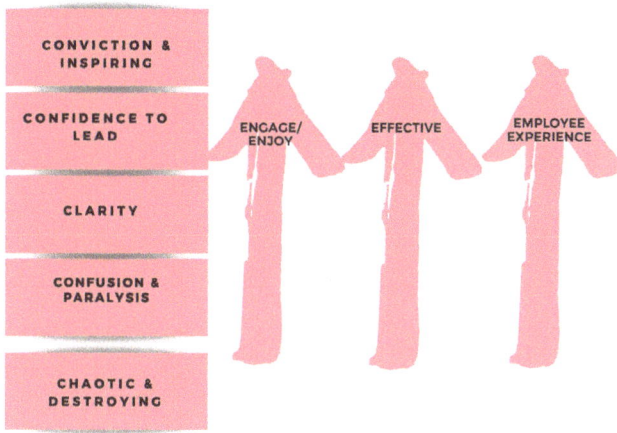

CONVICTION & INSPIRING

CONFIDENCE TO LEAD

CLARITY

CONFUSION & PARALYSIS

CHAOTIC & DESTROYING

ENGAGE/ENJOY

EFFECTIVE

EMPLOYEE EXPERIENCE

Leadership Development Model

How Can Women Step Into Their Power?

As you move through the Leadership Development Model, going up the ladder from chaos to conviction, you will find that you and the people around you (employees, clients, suppliers) will also start to shift. As you lead with clarity and confidence, you will start to enjoy your work more, you will feel more engaged in your work and you will notice you are using your time better because you are so focused. If you manage staff, you will also notice that you enhance their experience in the workplace. It's a win all 'round!

Women are doing exciting new things, taking greater chances and leaning in more than ever before. Women are also working longer hours and are more isolated. They urgently need to know their worth, be able to work on their terms and understand their potential.

How, then, do the most successful women break the glass ceiling, ensure they get paid their worth, and grow their businesses to their fullest potential?

The Three Elements Of Success

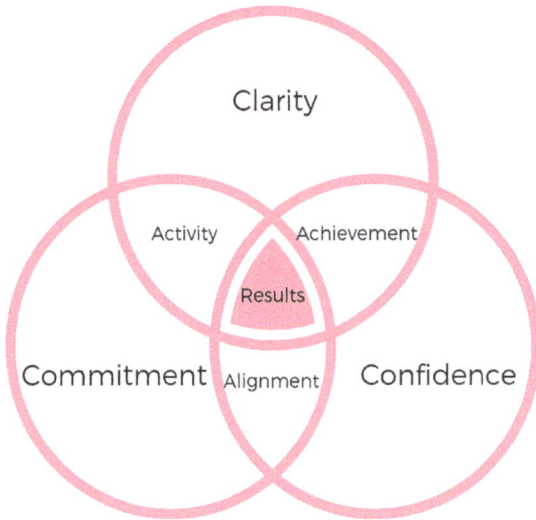

As we have explored, women have a lot to deal with: our inner critic, workplace barriers and stereotypes. But we can regain our mojo, shift our mindset and take back control.

There are three elements that create success: Clarity, Confidence and Commitment. Let's explore these critical elements in more detail.

1. Clarity

Without clarity, there is no success. Clarity allows passion and purpose to align. When there is a clear goal and clear steps, we can work towards success. For example, one of my clients came to me because she struggled with clarity. She had so many ideas and tried to do them all, but she then fell into overwhelm and none got done. We pared back her ideas, allowing her to only work with one idea at a time until it was ready to hit the market. Then, once that idea was up and running, we moved to the next idea. Her ideas were fabulous and worked well in the market, but working on them all at the same time was too much for her.

I see this play out within organisations as well. An executive team rolls out a new strategy. They put their voice to it – some of them articulate it well, others do not. The teams feel like they are not clear on what they need to do and, needless to say, not much gets done.

Clarity is like having a map: without it, we feel lost.

2. Confidence

Confidence is having belief in yourself. A leader needs the confidence to keep going when things are rough, to know when to change pace or pivot, and to succeed.

Confidence is like a magnet. We all want to be around someone who is confident; it makes us feel like anything is possible.

One of my clients struggled with confidence. It impacted her ability to get sales through the door. To help her, we delved into her natural strengths, and she started using those more. This enabled her to test things in a safe place. She began to put herself out there more and realised it wasn't as scary as she initially thought. You see, activity breeds confidence.

Do men struggle with self-confidence the same way women do? According to Laura Guillen, an Assistant Professor of Organisational Behaviour at ESMT Berlin, confidence is gender-neutral. However, she does state that "the consequences of appearing self-confident are not. The 'performance plus confidence equals power and influence' formula is gendered. Successful women cannot 'lean in' on a structure that cannot support their weight without their opportunities (and the myth) collapsing around them."[11]

According to an internal report from Hewlett Packard, women only apply for jobs in which they meet 100% of the criteria. Men apply if they think they meet 60% of the criteria. Women wait until they feel "ready", except we never feel ready.[12]

Yet, the research says we are as self-confident as men. How does this make any sense? Men are better at talking about the results than women. We hope that the results speak for themselves, yet they do not.

There's another interesting thing I have noted about confidence. The confident person in the room, the one who speaks up and "seems" confident, may not be the most competent in the room! Can we read that again? The confident person in the room *may not be the most competent person in the room.*

So, how does that work? According to Columbia Business School, men naturally (and rather honestly) "tilt toward overconfidence." Columbia Business School call this "honest overconfidence". To add fuel to this fire, they also found "that men on average rate their performance to be 30% better than it is."[13] This got me thinking about the executives I have worked with and the fact they were confident but actually not that competent. Yet it did not matter, especially when they hired smart people around them. Now, I am not saying they were not bright, just that their confidence came first and their competence came later.

3. Commitment

Commitment is being dedicated or using deliberate intent. It's about doing what you say you will do. Commitment means nothing if there is no follow-through. Once you are committed, you are fully "in".

I love this quote from former tennis ace Martina Navratilova: "The difference between involvement and commitment is like ham and eggs. The chicken is involved; the pig is committed."

Now, let's look at the intersections of Clarity, Commitment and Confidence:

- **Clarity + Commitment = Activity**

  You are crystal clear on what needs to happen, and you are highly committed to getting it done. Now is the time to decide what you need to do next. It's time to get on with it. When you focus on the *right* activity, with deliberate intent, success will follow. Having a plan and implementing the plan is what enables you to get stuff done.

- **Commitment + Confidence = Alignment**

  Alignment is like all the pieces of a puzzle coming together. You feel at peace because you know you are doing the right things, and you are focused on the end result.

  I had a client who was trying to sell some coaching packages. She was doing all the right things, she had the self-confidence, but her target market wasn't buying. After testing her service in a couple of different markets, we realised that if we turned the dial about 5% and changed her market slightly, she was onto a winning formula. She found alignment between her commitment and her confidence. And she has never looked back. She has now unlocked her potential.

- **Clarity + Confidence = Achievement**

  You feel the momentum pushing you forward. You are clear on your goals and you are confident about the path ahead. You start to achieve small wins, which has a snowball effect until, eventually, your goals are realised. This doesn't mean it's easy, but is anything worthwhile ever easy?

- **Clarity + Confidence + Commitment = Results (you are unstoppable!)**

When you achieve clarity, commitment and confidence, you get results. Results are what make us thrive as workers, leaders and business owners. They help us measure success and tell us we are on the right track.

One of my clients, Margaret, came to me exasperated that she was not getting results, even though she was doing the work. We did a deep dive into what she was doing. She didn't have the clarity required to do the tasks in front of her, she wasn't committed to her work, and she lacked the confidence to ask for help. No wonder she was in a state of disarray!

We put some simple things in place for her. One of these things was getting clarity from her boss. Since she had no idea what success looked like for one of her tasks, we agreed she would sit her boss down to ask how they would measure success and what success looked like for that task. This helped her get clear on the deliverable, which made it easier for her to ask for the help she needed. I checked in with her a month later, and she was on fire. Margaret had the clarity she needed, her commitment had returned, and because she knew exactly what she needed to do and had achieved some small wins, she had a renewed confidence that propelled her forward.

I liken getting results to that feeling you get when you've been looking for a specific pair of shoes. It's pure elation when you finally find them!

So, now that we've explored the three critical elements of success, let's bust some myths so you can raise your mojo, shift your mindset and thrive – and become a go-getter!

Myth #1:
"I should be happy with what I have."

We make deals with ourselves that we are happy where we are. We tell ourselves we have a good life, we should be satisfied with what we have, we should feel grateful for all the opportunities we have had and continue to have. After all, we live in the lucky country, right?

We think we should be happy "with a job" when we return from maternity leave. We think we should be grateful for the flexibility afforded to us (I don't disagree, but I do think that flexibility goes both ways). We think we are lucky to find that part-time role, because there are not many around. We settle for how we think things should be instead of really asking ourselves, "What could I improve in this to create a life I love?"

Do we *really* need to do that?

I worked with Sarah for two years. Sarah came to me in a state of disarray. She was working full time, parenting her two children, and had ageing parents who needed more and more care. Meanwhile, her siblings lived abroad, interstate or didn't seem to want to help.

Sarah was like most other women: she felt she should be happy with what she had. But the reality was, she was in a world of pain, suffocating from her obligations and resentful of her situation.

Sarah knew something needed to change, but she could not figure a way around her circumstances. If she stayed where she was, she felt she would crumble. Yet if she dropped her burdens, who would pick them up? What would happen to her mum and dad? After all, they were the priority, weren't they?

obligation
noun

- An act or course of action to which a person is morally or legally bound: a duty or commitment.
  "I have an obligation to look after her."

  synonyms: duty, commitment, responsibility, moral imperative.

- The condition of being morally or legally bound to do something.
  "They are under no obligation to stick to the scheme."

- A debt of gratitude for a service or favour.
  "She didn't want to be under an obligation to him."

  synonyms: contract, agreement, deed, covenant, bond, treaty, deal, pact, compact, understanding, transaction.

While this was Sarah's situation, I wonder how many of us feel like this? We get on with things because "that's the way it's supposed to be," without considering a new way, a better way to make it all work.

I worked with Sarah on shifting her mindset from one of obligation, responsibility and resentment, to one of care, compassion and boundaries.

Here is what we did for Sarah specifically:

- **We listed the things that were important to her and put them in order of priority**

   Creating a list of things that were important to Sarah was the first step in untangling what she considered the "mess of life". Putting them into an order of priority was a great way to work out where she should focus her energy.

- **We worked out the pain points**

   Delving into each task and working out the pain points was, as Sarah said, "cathartic" (and it meant we could identify what could help). It gave her the clarity to get into a practical headspace.

- **We made a list of things we could ditch, outsource or delegate, and keep**

   We had three buckets: tasks to ditch because they no longer served Sarah; tasks to outsource or delegate (and to whom); and, lastly, tasks to keep (yes, keep was deliberately last).

- **We put an action plan in place**

What transpired from all that work were several conversations with the people around Sarah, Sarah's own work on her mindset, and Sarah holding on to the boundaries she had put into place. The plan was broken into the three buckets: tasks to ditch, tasks to outsource or delegate, and tasks to keep. The outsource or delegate bucket included having a conversation with her immediate family about the situation she was in, and asking them to take some of the pieces. For instance, one of her children agreed to prepare dinner twice a week, and the other agreed to take on the laundry as their commitment. She also researched where she could find some additional services in her community to help her parents.

resentment
noun

- Bitter indignation at having been treated unfairly.
  "His resentment at being demoted."

  synonyms: bitterness, indignation, irritation, pique, displeasure, dissatisfaction, disgruntlement, discontentment, discontent, resentfulness, bad feelings, hard feelings, ill feelings, acrimony, rancour, animosity, hostility, jaundice, antipathy, antagonism, enmity, hatred, hate.

As women, we tend to feel our sense of obligation and responsibility at a deep level. This may be because we have been brought up to feel this way, or we have taken on more responsibility than we needed to. Eventually, this turns into resentment, and no one wants to live there.

In her book, *Girl, Wash Your Face*, Rachel Hollis says, "You, and only you, are ultimately responsible for who you become and how happy you are."[14]

The trouble is, sometimes we don't know how to get out of that rut. Once Sarah was able to identify the things that were important to her and put them in order of priority, she was able to come up with solutions and an action plan to help her live a happier, less overwhelming life.

Is that the end of the story? Of course not. Will it take discipline and consistency to stay on track? Of course it will! Sarah is committed because she knows her new way of doing things will help her immensely.

Sometimes, you just need to work through the "mess of life" and get clear on your priorities.

There are so many definitions of happiness, but the one I love the most is from Positive Psychology researcher Sonja Lyubomirsky, who describes it as "the experience of joy, contentment, or positive well-being, combined with a sense that one's life is good, meaningful and worthwhile."[15]

happiness
noun

- The state of being happy.
  "She struggled to find happiness in her life."

  synonyms: contentment, pleasure, contentedness, satisfaction, cheerfulness, cheeriness, merriment, gaiety, joy, joyfulness, joyousness, joviality, jollity, jolliness, glee, blitheness, carefreeness, gladness, delight, good spirits, high spirits, light-heartedness, good cheer, wellbeing, enjoyment, felicity.

So, what are the qualities of a happy person? Martin Seligman, founder of Positive Psychology, uses the acronym PERMA to represent the five qualities that contribute to happiness:[16]

P: Positive emotions (enjoying yourself in the moment).
E: Engagement (losing track of time and becoming completely absorbed in an activity we enjoy).
R: Relationships (having deep, meaningful relationships with others is vital to our wellbeing).
M: Meaning (dedicating ourselves to a cause or recognising something bigger than ourselves).
A: Achievement (we thrive when we achieve our goals).

How do you think you rate on these five qualities? Are there areas where you would like to improve so you can be more happy?

"I should be happy with what I have."

What Happens When You Are Too Nice?

We can't do it all. Sometimes, we need help – even as leaders.

Since working for myself, I have struggled to put into words the things I need when I have sought help from a third party. I know what I need to do to get the job done, but there are no mind readers out there! I have had to work that little bit harder to explain very clearly what I need.

Two of the biggest things I am guilty of when communicating with people is assuming they know more than they do, and that they can read my mind. How often have you been guilty of making these assumptions?

When asking for help, the easiest ways to avoid confusion and provide clarity are to:

- Never make assumptions about people's knowledge. Have open discussions about what they already know and what they need to know.

- Never think a person can read your mind (as great as it would be if they could!). You need to clearly communicate all the information they need and be direct with your requests (bearing in mind that the person you're asking for help may need more information than you do).

The impact of making assumptions is that it leads to confusion and things don't get done correctly, if at all.

Another key consideration is how clear you are about your requirements and expectations. Lack of clarity around these is a common trap for women who don't want to upset other people. We often want to come across as "nice" all the time, and we can sometimes mistake being direct for being unpleasant.

If you desire to be "nice", it's not about the message you are trying to get across, but the way you communicate it. I truly believe you can be kind and communicate clearly in business.

Here are three things that will ensure you are clear about your requirements and expectations while being kind:

1. Work on the relationship first and foremost and ensure both parties understand each other's intention. Having said that, we tend to judge a person's actions rather than their intent, so make sure your actions align with your intent.

2. Talk about what would happen for each of you when you're under stress – before a stressful situation arises. Discuss how you would deal with it so, when the time comes, you can say, "I am under a bit of stress at the moment," or, "I can see you are struggling at the moment, what can I do to help?"

3. When you make a mistake, admit it, apologise, talk about it and move on.

Take the time to ensure the person you are communicating with understands your expectations. Again, do not assume their knowledge or that they can read your mind. Having these discussions in the first instance provides clarity and understanding. By being clear and direct, we ensure everyone is on the same page and that we are getting the things we need.

So, next time you need something from someone, be clear about expectations and timelines. Help them out, which in turn helps you.

Truth #1:

There is more (that you want to do and can do)

We all want more energy, confidence and financial freedom. Now is the time. We know that unless we step into our careers or business, we will remain stagnant. The good news is this: there *is* more out there for you, but you have to really want it, and you have to be prepared to work *in the right way* for it. You need to be ready to do something different to get there.

Women who go out, grab life with two hands and give it a red-hot go appreciate what they have, and they go and get more. They have a bunch of like-minded women supporting them on their journey.

Passion + Purpose = Fulfilment

When we feel passionate about what we are doing, the hours fly by. We feel energised in our work and others see our "spark".

Think about those people you meet who you know are in the right job. They have a genuine love for what they do and look forward to Monday morning. You can see that their passion and purpose are aligned and they feel fulfilled. They are in their sweet spot, where results happen, because they are playing to their strengths.

Are you someone who has found their passion and purpose? Or is this something you are still searching for?

There is a misconception that finding passion and purpose is only an issue for people starting out in their careers. I find that for some of my clients, it is more of a problem for those stuck in a job or business they don't enjoy.

Finding your passion is easier for some people than others. Many people finish their studies and find themselves in roles they had been advised were the best for them based on their academic results, but sadly, they aren't passionate about these jobs. Or they are promoted within an organisation but don't find themselves aligned with the core values of the organisation.

Some people know in their heart of hearts what their driving force is. Others are unsure but know what they are currently doing is not their passion.

When trying to determine what your passion is, think about something you feel compelled to do, something that sits with you and leaves you with strong emotions. If this doesn't work, think about what you have always wanted to do, or the things you always wanted to do or achieve when you "grew up".

"Follow your passion.
It will lead you to your purpose."

Oprah Winfrey

Our purpose is the reason why we do something. When we work with a purpose, we feel content and aligned.

You know how it feels when your back is out: you can barely function, moving is difficult, you get headaches, you can't sleep or eat properly, nothing feels right. It isn't until you go to the chiropractor and get realigned that you get a sense of relief and you can function properly again.

The same can be said about purpose. When you don't have purpose or you are not aligned with your purpose, nothing else works. You are unmotivated, it can be difficult to concentrate and commit to what you are doing, and generally, you are not happy. It is not until you find your purpose and are aligned with it that you can function to your full potential.

Finding your purpose means figuring out why you are here. For some people, it is about finding a job that allows them to excel in their chosen field. For others, it may be finding a job that allows them to balance their need to focus on other areas of their life (parenting, volunteering, nurturing their mental and physical wellbeing).

Whatever your passion and purpose, you need to be true to yourself.

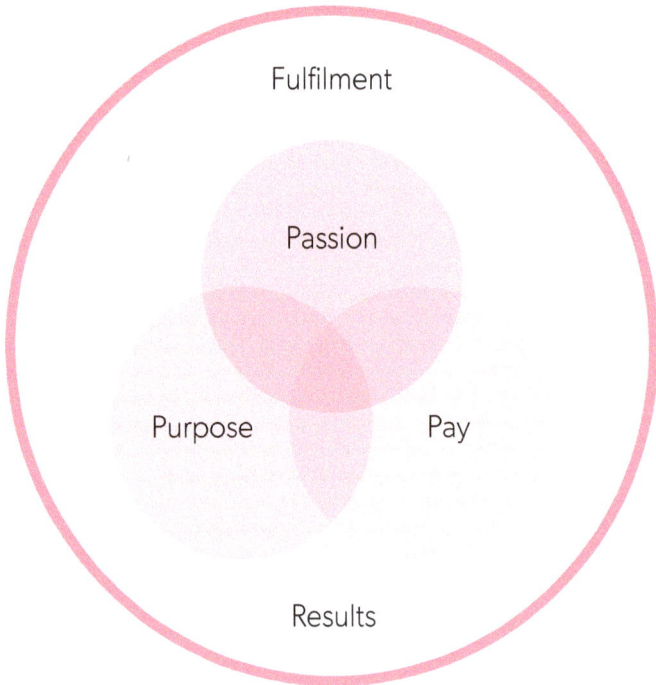

The Sweet Spot

It's hard to get up every day if you know your passion and purpose don't align with the work you do.

Let me share with you one of my all-time favourite stories about a client who knew her passion and purpose were not aligned and did everything in her power to ensure they were.

Lauren was in a sales job. She knew it wasn't the job for her. She was selling training and development solutions, but something was missing. What was missing was her ability to help people and mix in her other love – YOGA!

So, Lauren and I started working together. We looked for a role that would incorporate her love of yoga and allow her to help people. Lauren went on a deep dive of discovery and found the perfect role for her: a recruitment adviser at a well-known yoga brand. Actually, Lauren didn't find the role; she networked extremely hard and demonstrated how much she wanted to be a part of the business. After a few months of doing all she could, she was offered the role. Now, her passion and purpose align perfectly.

So, have you found your passion and purpose?

Keep. Stop. Start.

After reading this chapter, think deeply and ask yourself:

What do I need to **KEEP** doing?

_____

_____

_____

What do I need to **STOP** doing?

_____

_____

_____

What do I need to **START** doing?

_____

_____

_____

Myth #2:

"I just need more time."

"If I only had more time. If there were more hours in the day, I could get that done."

Society doesn't help with this one. We constantly hear references to time running out, lack of time, having "no time". *"I have too much to do and not enough time,"* we all whisper to ourselves at one point or another (I'm guilty of this, too!).

I hear this ALL the time. This is especially true for business owners starting out. It feels like there is never enough time in the day, there is too much to do, we are impatient for results (again, I was one of these people, too). This has become a universal "truth".

But it's also true that Jacinda Ardern only has 86,400 seconds in a day. Greta Thunberg only has 86,400 seconds in a day – and she travels internationally by boat! Beyoncé only has 86,400 seconds in the day. And so do you.

Truth #2:

There is no more time

Imagine, if you will, an hourglass. It holds 24 hours only. We all have the same sized hourglass. Therefore, everything we choose to do must fit into 24 hours, including:

- Time for you to nourish yourself, sleep well and be fit for each day.
- Time for the people who are closest to you.
- Time for the work you love to do, making the difference you were born to make.

The most successful women in business and leadership ruthlessly prioritise. They know how to distinguish the important from the urgent, and how to balance both. And when they don't, they have someone in their corner to gently (or loudly) keep them on track.

Managing The Minutes

Everyone has the same 86,400 seconds/1,440 minutes/ 24 hours in a day. But why is it that some people seem to get more out of their time than others?

A simple yet effective technique I use to get the most out of my time is the Pomodoro Technique. The Pomodoro Technique teaches you to work with time instead of against it.

Developed in the late 1980s by entrepreneur Francesco Cirillo, the Pomodoro Technique (named after the tomato-shaped kitchen timer that Cirillo used) uses a timer to break work into intervals.

There are six steps to this technique:

1. **Choose a task you would like to get done**

   This can be any task you wish – small, big, easy, hard, something that has just landed, or something you have been putting off for ages. Anything!

2. **Set the Pomodoro (timer) for 25 minutes**

   Don't allow yourself to be tempted by the usual distractions in this 25-minute interval. You know the ones I'm talking about! Set the phone to silent and don't look at those emails.

3. **Work on the task until the Pomodoro rings**

   Turn 100% of your focus to the task at hand. If another thought pops into your head, jot it down on a piece of paper to come back to later, and refocus immediately.

4. **When the Pomodoro rings, put a checkmark on paper**

   Yay! You did it! An entire uninterrupted interval on a task!

5. **Take a short break**

   Give yourself five minutes to stand up, stretch, go for a short walk or grab a coffee.

6. **Every four Pomodoro intervals, take a longer break**

   Once you have completed four Pomodoros, take a longer break of 20 to 30 minutes – long enough to feel recharged and ready to start another 25-minute work session.

Repeat this process over the course of a workday and you will be amazed at how much you can accomplish!

How To Manage Distractions

So, you have the Pomodoro Technique, but what are you meant to do about those unavoidable distractions? You know the ones – meetings, co-workers, emergencies. When possible, Cirillo suggests postponing the distraction until the Pomodoro is complete using the "inform, negotiate, schedule, call back" strategy outlined below:[17]

1. **Inform** the other (distracting) party that you're working on something right now.

2. **Negotiate** a time when you can get back to them about the distracting issue in a timely manner.

3. **Schedule** that follow-up immediately.

4. **Call back** the other party when your Pomodoro is complete and you're ready to tackle their issue.

Using this strategy, you will find your use of the Pomodoro Technique will improve when those unexpected distractions arise.

Keep. Stop. Start.

After reading this chapter, think deeply and ask yourself:

What do I need to **KEEP** doing?

_____

_____

_____

What do I need to **STOP** doing?

_____

_____

_____

What do I need to **START** doing?

_____

_____

_____

Myth #3:

"It shouldn't be this hard."

You may be asking yourself, "How do I level up at work? The feedback I'm receiving is telling me to step up, but I don't know what stepping up means. How do I work out what I'm doing well that I can leverage? What skills do I need to build?"

You may have been working for several years in an organisation or for yourself. You have been running for what feels like a long time. You are good at what you do, but you feel unappreciated and unrewarded for your work.

Women who have their own businesses or are in leadership positions do not seem to have enough time in the day to get everything done. They don't make the money they know they deserve. They're juggling family and business, feeling overwhelmed and unsure of what the next steps are. Many women in these positions feel busy but not productive. Everything feels so hard.

You may be asking yourself, "How can I do work that I love and make money out of this business idea?"

You may have watched your friends or colleagues and know they work their guts out but don't seem to be benefiting from it. In fact, they're going backwards. It's like they've stepped onto a treadmill and the treadmill is in reverse!

You may have slowly climbed the corporate ladder and have somehow come to a standstill. It may be that you have chosen not to go any further, that the season in your life isn't right, or that with all your competing priorities, it just can't be your career right now.

Are You Losing Your Mind?

Now, the following may not directly apply to some of you – but please don't let that stop you reading. You see, I am going to talk about the mental load mothers face when blending motherhood and work.

For those of you who feel this does not apply to you, I plead with you to read on, as I can assure you, it does apply to you. I have no doubt you have a working mother in your life in some capacity – whether she is your partner, sister, work colleague or a friend. Please read this and think of them.

One of the hardest parts of the mental load is that often it is not shared. This results in women feeling like they have to deal with this burden themselves. However, the reality is there are roles so many of us can play in easing the mental load for those around us.

"We expect women to work like they have no children and raise children as though they don't work."

Anonymous

It sounds ridiculous, but the above quote is a reality many working mothers face, whether they work full time, part time or on a casual basis, or run their own business.

I returned to work seven months after giving birth to my youngest daughter. At the time, my other daughters were 13 and 14 years old. I had no choice but to return to work in a full-time capacity as I was the breadwinner for the family while my husband was studying to pursue a career change.

I intended to take 12 months of maternity leave, but on my boss's request, I returned to work after seven months to lead a special transformational project looking after approximately 20 people. It is fair to say the environment I returned to was quite hostile and the people I worked with did not want me there (so many good stories about how *not* to behave!).

As a result of this environment, I felt the need to work harder and beyond the contracted hours. I found myself taking work home. On many occasions, I would start early or finish late, taking calls and having work creep into my personal time – the time I was meant to dedicate to my family. I couldn't keep on top of all the things that needed to be done in the multiple areas of my life.

I felt guilty at work because I was away from my family. I felt guilty because I was thinking about my family while on the clock. I felt guilty at home because of the pressure to work during my family time. I felt like I was constantly chasing my tail and found it incredibly difficult to juggle everything.

The mental load for women and mothers is huge. The mental load of blending motherhood and work is next level!

What does the mental load look like? It's all the things that we, as women and mothers, take responsibility for.

It's constantly thinking about your family and their needs; arranging logistics to make sure all the kids get to school, day care and extracurricular activities; ensuring the shopping list has been written, the shopping has been done, a meal plan arranged; making sure the kids' immunisations and doctor appointments are up to date; keeping on top of your "paid" work and not dropping the ball; making sure the family has clean clothes to wear; paying the bills; organising Christmas presents for the kids and extended family… the list goes on (and never ends). The list is always on our minds and continually added to, even when we are at capacity.

Don't get me wrong, I love the work I do (especially now!). I love motherhood more than anything, and I understand it will be a juggle from time to time, but my goodness, the mental load can be so draining!

Many are quick to point out that the majority of partners do their fair share of the household chores, and yes, this can be true. But household chores and the mental load are two very different things.

For whatever reason, be it gender-stereotyped roles, be it different genetic make-up, men don't seem to take on the mental load to the same extent as women, if at all. As a result, women often feel the task of carrying the mental load falls with them.

So, what can we do to alleviate the mental load for working mothers?

• **Set boundaries**

    Technology means people are "switched on" and "available" almost 24/7. In generations before us, once you left your workplace, you were finished for the day and could switch your focus to your family. Now, with smartphones and email, the ability to switch off is almost impossible. Instead of leaving your workplace, you often take a portion of your work home with you. It is important to set boundaries to ensure work does not take over your personal life.

• **Have difficult conversations**

    This can be a tricky one, but it is important to have difficult conversations with people, particularly around boundaries. Unfortunately, there is still the expectation within organisations that working mothers should work as though they have no children. I have heard of women returning to work part time, contracted for three days per week, but due to organisational expectations, they also worked for two unpaid days per week to keep up with the demand of their role (so, practically full time).

• **Manage your expectations**

No doubt you have high expectations of yourself. You need to manage these expectations and cut yourself some slack. You are only capable of so much, and that's okay. Not everything has to be perfect. One of my favourite mottos is "done is better than perfect." It's okay if you didn't have the chance to do the grocery shopping and the kids had toast and tinned spaghetti for dinner – it's not like you didn't feed them at all, is it? And, in all seriousness, chances are they ate it with no fuss and enjoyed it more than a meal you could have put hours of effort into and they wouldn't eat!

"Done is better than perfect."

Emma McQueen

• **Build your tribe**

The role of a mother can be isolating. The role of a working mum even more so. It is almost like you don't fit into the mum circle or the work circle; you are stuck between the two. Reach out and build your tribe. Connect with other working mums, connect with your colleagues, connect with mums in your area and reach out to friends and family. It takes a village to raise a child, so build yours.

- **Ask for help and take offers of help**

  Asking for help can be so difficult. For some reason, women fear judgement from society (unfortunately, mostly from other women) if it seems they are not coping. This fear of judgement needs to stop. Everyone is doing the best they can. If you need help, ask for it. And if someone is kind enough to offer you help (that is actually going to be helpful), don't be afraid to take it. A small note on this: when you accept someone's help, they will not do things *exactly* the same way you would (including our families!). Be okay with that, be happy with the help and the outcome, and don't stress about the "how" – it's just not worth it.

- **Don't expect people to read your mind**

  This one is tricky. Just because you have a mental load doesn't necessarily mean your partner does. They may not know you are burdened by the mental load, as it's not visible (unless you have reached breaking point). You need to communicate this with them.

- **Outsource what you can**

  I know you want to, but you simply cannot do everything or be everything to everyone. If you can outsource, do so. There are so many new businesses that offer amazing services for almost anything you can think of. Caroline Guillemain-Brunne and her team at Organise.Curate. Design.[18] offer a Life Assistant service (who doesn't want one of those?!), and they do an amazing job of helping mums and dads work through their priorities and clear the mental clutter at an affordable price. One of the decisions I made last year was to get some help with my wardrobe, as deciding what to wear every morning was a killer for my brain. Nicole Vine Personal Stylist[19] made this process super easy for me, and the best bit? I have a "look book" I can open on my phone where my outfits are styled and ready to go. This small thing has changed my life!

• **Be kind**

Be kind to yourself – you are doing the best you can. Extend this kindness to other working mothers. Don't judge – you know yourself how tough this gig can be, so no doubt it is tough for many others.

So, to all my fellow working mummas, "I hear you, I see you, I am you."

Truth #3:

It is hard work, but you can amplify the result

While the word "hustle" has grown to have a negative connotation, success does require a little hustle. Even more, it requires you to get a bit uncomfortable.

As humans, we are neurologically wired to find our comfort zone and do whatever we can to protect it. The truth is, growth and comfort cannot co-exist. To grow, we need to do things we have not done before, in ways we have not done before, which feels uncomfortable.

The most successful women have someone in their corner, expanding their limitations on what is possible and helping them identify areas of discomfort worth leaning into.

How Do You Show Up?

Does this sound familiar? You have had a rough morning and feel like you have done a million things to get the family ready before your "work" day even starts. Your day is full: back-to-back meetings with clients, deadlines and all the typical daily tasks. You feel overwhelmed and wonder how you will summon the energy to get through the day.

We have all had days like these (some more than others!), and we need to decide how we show up. Do we show up exhausted, ungrateful and scatterbrained? Or do we show up and choose to be present with whoever we are meeting with?

Too often, I see people not showing up. Their energy is lacking, they complain about what's happening with them, and they are generally a drag to be around. Now, please don't get me wrong, everyone has bad days, and that's fine, but I urge you to be aware of how you show up and what it means for those around you.

So, why aren't people showing up? This is a good question, and the answer is different for everyone. However, the most common reasons I hear are:

- **Too many things in our brain box**

  We all play a number of roles in our everyday lives, including parent, partner, boss/employee, friend… the list goes on. Each of these roles comes with so many things we need to think about and do. For some people, when things get too much, the automatic response is to shut down and not show up.

- **Can't be bothered**

  This is a big one. We all seem to be running at such a fast pace, which results in the feeling of utter exhaustion. When we have nothing left in the tank, the simplest of tasks can feel like mammoth ones. In these instances, it's easy not to show up properly or even at all.

- **Overwhelmed**

   The numerous roles we play and the heavy workload that comes with each can bring a massive sense of overwhelm, which has a significant impact on our ability to show up. Is it time to say no to some things?

The consequences of not showing up are substantial and can have an ongoing negative impact on us:

- **Work compounds**

   If you don't show up, workloads get bigger. Unfortunately, the work doesn't go away and given the general reasons for not showing up (see above), in some instances, it can result in the work expanding to the point of no return.

- **People notice – and notice us for the wrong reasons**

   It is obvious to people when you are not showing up. People are perceptive, and they notice the energy we bring with us. If you bring negative energy to what you do, people will avoid you.

- **A bad reputation**

   People are quick to judge and form an impression of you. If you are not showing up, chances are, their impression of you will not be a good one and, unfortunately, they are likely to tell others of their experience with you. A bad reputation can create irreversible damage to your career/ business.

The above being said, when we do show up, it can lead to amazing things.

I want to tell you about a client of mine who consistently shows up. She is amazeballs! Dani is a senior business leader in her community. She runs a number of businesses and sits on two boards. She also has three children and the normal issues around running a busy household.

Several years ago, one of her businesses was not doing terribly well, so I was working with her to turn it around. She had to pivot her business, as her industry was in turmoil and she knew if she didn't change something, she would no longer have a business.

We were due to meet at 10am. Overnight, Dani had received some interesting (read: bad) media, and she was fielding calls from reporters and the business world, all wanting to speak with her.

The things that impressed me were:

1. She showed up to the session (I would have fully forgiven her if she hadn't shown up that day).
2. She was present and focused throughout the session.
3. She did not take a call or look at her phone the entire time we were together.

Within six months, Dani had turned her business around and managed to keep all her talent and turn a profit. I have no doubt the outcome was so positive because of the way she showed up, time and time again. My experience with Dani was similar each time we met. She was consistent with how she showed up.

So, the critical question is: what can we do to ensure we are showing up?

I know I talk about self-care and mindset a lot, and the reason is that they are both so important. You need to ensure you are looking after yourself so you can show up when needed.

Some of the things I do to ensure I look after myself and, in turn, show up are:

- Allow time between meetings and, if possible, arrange meetings away from my place of work so I can walk to and from the meeting. I find that pre-meeting, this gives me time to set myself up for the meeting, and post-meeting, it allows time to reflect and reset for my return to the office. As a bonus, I get some fresh air and sunlight on my walk.

- Book an hour a week with myself to sit, reflect, think and journal (and keep that appointment!).

- Use 10 minutes a day to practise mindfulness: slow my breathing, slow my pace and appreciate what is around me. I find doing this after the craziness of the family morning routine and before my "work" day starts helps me set a positive mindset for the day ahead.

- Get up at the same time each morning and go to bed at the same time each night. We all thrive on routine and regular sleep is key.

- Turn off all technology an hour before bed. This goes hand in hand with the above point. Switching off technology before bed and not looking at it as soon as you wake up gives you better sleep and a clear mind.

- Focus on one thing at a time. We all have so much going on in our lives, but it is important not to get overwhelmed by it all. Make a list and prioritise. Focusing on one thing at a time ensures we are more effective in achieving what we need to, rather than being busy yet not accomplishing anything.

- Play to your strengths. Don't try to be all things to all people. Focus on your strengths and delegate or outsource the tasks that don't bring joy or you know are better suited to others.

- Know your peaks and troughs. Everyone has natural energy cycles throughout the day. Think carefully about your cycle, pinpointing times when you feel more focused and productive, and use these times to your advantage.

- Build your "no" muscle. Learning to say no is like anything else – it's hard to do to at first but gets progressively easier with practice.

Keep. Stop. Start.

After reading this chapter, think deeply and ask yourself:

What do I need to **KEEP** doing?

_____

_____

_____

What do I need to **STOP** doing?

_____

_____

_____

What do I need to **START** doing?

_____

_____

_____

Myth #4:

"I need the world to stop so I can catch up."

Being in chaos is one of the most unproductive states to be in. It decreases our effectiveness and increases our stress response state, further inhibiting our performance. On top of that, it puts relationships at risk – at an employee level, a client level and a supplier level.

No one wants to be stuck in chaos. It feels like you have too many plates spinning at once, threatening to fall. Not to mention how exhausting it is for you and everyone around you.

Do you find yourself in a constant state of limbo? Juggling all the different parts of your life – work, family, friends, health, etc.? Whether you are a small business owner, manager, leader or employee, the juggling act is constant and tiring.

Several years ago, Brian Dyson, the then president and CEO of Coca-Cola Enterprises, delivered a speech in which he discussed the difference between glass and rubber balls:[20]

"Imagine life as a game in which you are juggling some five balls in the air. You name them – work, family, health, friends and spirit – and you're keeping all of these in the air. You will soon understand that work is a rubber ball. If you drop it, it will bounce back. But the other four balls – family, health, friends and spirit – are made of glass. If you drop one of these, they will be irrevocably scuffed, marked, nicked, damaged or even shattered. They will never be the same. You must understand that and strive for balance in your life."

Striving for balance in your life, as Dyson suggests, is something often much easier said than done. The kind of balance that keeps the glass balls from breaking and the rubber ball from bouncing will look different for everyone. What is important is recognising your priorities and working with them accordingly.

The balancing act is one that took some time for me to master (I say "master" with tongue in cheek!), but I believe no matter what level of balance you are trying to achieve, these tips can help. I have put all these tips into place over the past 12 months, and I can honestly say they work!

1. **Schedule important personal activities**

    These are the things that can quickly fall by the wayside if they aren't scheduled purposefully. Exercise, date nights, catching up with friends – these are all important. Block time in your calendar for these personal activities and you will find they happen as they should.

2. Set boundaries

Set firm boundaries around when you are and aren't available. Doing so will help you relax when you are off the clock and help others avoid unmet expectations.

3. Unplug

Designate a certain amount of time to "unplug" yourself from your mobile phone and the internet. These things keep you hooked to work and useless activities that prevent you from engaging in the important ones, like getting enough rest, spending quality time with the people you connect with and participating in things that make you happy and help you relax.

Striving for balance is a continuous process that requires reflection and adaptation to meet your changing needs.

Truth #4:

You can move from chaos to calm - it's a choice

You know you need to get out of chaos. This is the first step – recognising the state you are in and starting to create a plan that will get you out.

As you work through your "escape plan", you will discover a new pain. It's called confusion. You feel like you are swimming through treacle. You know you are on track to getting out of the chaos, but you start to realise how much needs to be done and it can become overwhelming. You sit in paralysis because you are not sure what to tackle, let alone how and when and in what order.

How do I know? We have all been there. Yes, even me!

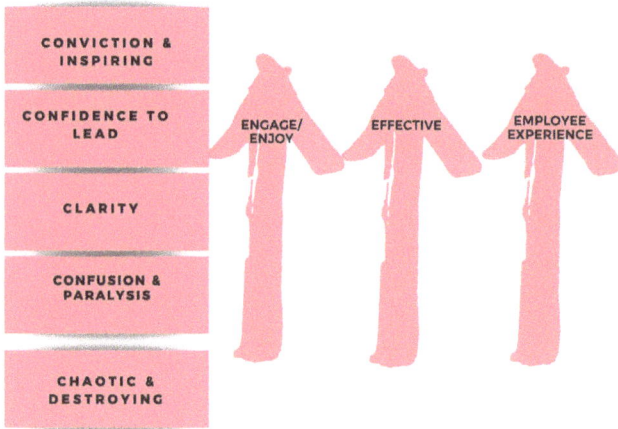

Leadership Development Model

Remember the Leadership Development Model? We need to move from a state of chaos to conviction and inspiration. It's true, it's not always easy and it takes time, but you can move up the ladder to achieve maximum engagement, enjoyment, effectiveness and a positive employee experience.

Let me tell you about Jasmine. She was in a painful position. Her business had grown too quickly, she had just split with her business partner, the finances looked like she was about to go bankrupt and she had ever-increasing business costs. She was busy working *in* her business rather than focusing *on* it. Doing nothing was not an option if she wanted to stay in business. She came to the realisation that her situation was not sustainable, so she worked incredibly hard to move away from being busy (and I can tell you, it is an ongoing challenge). She employed some excellent strategies and enlisted the necessary support, and has since made significant steps towards creating the life she wants.

Sometimes, escaping the chaos feels as though you're wading through mud. You start to get some wins on the board – if you pull this lever here, it will have an impact there, and you begin to focus on what's really important to your success. You have days when you think, "Yes, I nailed that," but you don't want to get too cocky, because it wasn't long ago that you were in chaos and confusion, and you know you could go back there at any moment. It's about being in the moment, realising, "Wow, I am enjoying the work, I am engaged, I feel in control and I know what the next steps are." You become effective and the people around you have an enjoyable experience with you because of your new-found clarity.

"It all starts with your mindset."

Emma McQueen

You Are The Boss – Or Are You?

Natalie has built a business that others would be envious of. Her company has approximately 20 employees, and she holds all the risk. She is the one stressing about people getting paid, having enough money in the bank, ensuring enough business comes through the door and that everyone is happy.

Natalie also has someone in the business in a day-to-day way – her manager, Paul. He looks after the everyday running of the place and does a superb job for Natalie.

When Paul started, Natalie warmly invited him into her business. He took ownership, cleared things up and made sure everyone was happy.

But then something changed. Paul started to have stronger opinions about the company. He also worked ridiculous hours, which meant Natalie felt like she had to as well. In fact, he started acting as though he owned the business. Natalie started to feel a power struggle. She was the business owner, yet she felt her company was being run by someone else.

It can be lonely in business, can't it? When we employ people to help us, we hand over some of our control. We talk to them about our decisions, and they become invaluable assets. But what happens when they overstep the mark? What happens when their bias gets in the way, when they stop making decisions at a commercial level, and you are no longer aligned?

Natalie had to reset her expectations and boundaries. She had to learn to say "this is okay" or "this is not okay". She had to grab her power back so she could continue to run her business.

This situation doesn't only impact business owners. It can also happen when you are the leader of a department or organisation, and your right-hand person feels they own the role as much as you.

Here's what Natalie and I did:

1. We unpacked all the issues: what was happening, why it was so, how it had come to this, what events had led to it, Natalie's role in it, Paul's role in it, and how it had made Natalie feel. She owned a lot of the issues. Once all the problems were on the table, it was easier to find a way forward.

2. We looked at all options, such as: maybe it was time for Paul to leave the business to reduce his voice; Natalie could ignore his voice and hope it would go away (it never does); or Natalie could have a clear and courage-filled conversation with him.

3. We decided on key themes. We role-played the conversations and how they may play out, what response we might get, how we would deal with it and what the fallout might be. One thing we knew for sure, Paul was an integral part of the business, but the power had shifted so significantly, we could no longer ignore it, nor did we want to lose Paul. It's a fine line, isn't it?

What we didn't do was list Paul's negative traits. This was a person who had been instrumental in setting this business up – he felt like he owned the company and was behaving accordingly. Wouldn't we all love employees who had this much skin in the game?

Has this ever happened to you? Have you had employees who have so much skin in the game that the lines of authority start to blur? Have you had to have that awkward conversation and be clear with them?

The conversation was awkward, filled with tears and apologies. They cleared the air on a number of things that had been misinterpreted over the course of their time working together, and they put in place processes to ensure this didn't happen again. To this day, Natalie still works hard to ensure she has control over the business and consults where necessary, but she realises that she is the boss and she needs to step into her power. Business is booming and they have doubled in size – no small feat! And Natalie, well, she is great at those conversations now!

Keep. Stop. Start.

After reading this chapter, think deeply and ask yourself:

What do I need to **KEEP** doing?

_____

_____

_____

What do I need to **STOP** doing?

_____

_____

_____

What do I need to **START** doing?

_____

_____

_____

emma McQUEEN

Myth #5:

"I should be able to do it on my own."

We crave connection. Women, men, children – we all want a relationship. But in a world of increasing disconnect, this can be hard to find. There are so many ways to connect now and yet, we feel lonelier than we have ever felt.

Research shows that loneliness poses such significant health risks, it carries a higher risk of premature death than smoking or obesity.[21] In fact, many nations across the world suggest we are facing a loneliness epidemic.

As women, we work as hard as the next person (let's be honest, we probably work a little harder as we break through barriers). We hope our work speaks for itself, yet deep down, we know it doesn't. That is me, that is you, that is all of us at some point or another.

When you put your idea out there or dared to start something new, no doubt everyone was encouraging and told you, "You've got this," and, "You can do it," and you can.

The problem is, it's lonely going it alone. When you leave an organisation, you leave the politics and bureaucracy behind, but what you also leave is the security of processes and procedures, a stable income and being part of a team. You are, literally, financially and emotionally, on your own.

Loneliness In Business

The first year in my business full time, I worked exceptionally hard and kicked lots of goals, but it was lonely. I mean really lonely, in ways I never expected.

When you step out of an organisation to pursue your own business, it's just you. You are reliant on yourself to make the decisions. I find that invigorating because I can change direction as easily and quickly as I like, but not having someone to bounce ideas off can be tough. You've got to look for that support system. You can't do it all on your own.

What if you don't find like-minded people to discuss ideas with? I'm not sure about you, but when I wasn't connected with like-minded people, I felt I couldn't test my ideas in a way that helped refine them. You know the old saying, "Two heads are better than one?" Well, I reckon about five heads are better than one!

Here are three simple steps I used to overcome the loneliness and get help:

1. I found like-minded people

I looked hard to find "my kind of people". This took a lot more time than I had anticipated, and I found them in the most unexpected of places. The list of characteristics I was looking for was not huge, but there was a list. I looked for people who were kind, honest, believed community over competition was best, were driven to achieve, and were open to a relationship with me.

There are various avenues you can use to find your people: local small business networks, co-working spaces and online communities and forums, such as Facebook groups. These are all great networking options and can be niche to specific industries or locations.

2. I sought advice from people ahead of me

I sought people who were a couple of years ahead of me in their business. This was important, as they had "been there, done that" and could guide me. I have a few business mentors now and each offers advice on various areas of my business.

3. I asked for help

Asking for help was difficult for me. I am self-sufficient, so I struggled with this, but you know what? I just needed to get over myself and put it out there when I needed the help.

Feeling Connected Versus Feeling Disconnected And Isolated

As stated at the start of this chapter, there's an epidemic – it's called loneliness.

But is it that we're lonely, or do we allow ourselves to become hermits?

One of my clients, Lisa, struggled with feeling isolated. She worked so hard that she didn't make time to connect with people. She didn't reach out to her network or ask for help. She was "head down, bum up."

Lisa hadn't taken the time to reach out to people in a meaningful way. She had become a bit of a hermit. She was absorbed in a whole new world of business, which she loved, but it meant she had isolated herself and had forgotten to stop and smell the roses, so to speak.

Lisa was lonely, really lonely. We all need people who have our backs, who are our cheerleaders, our supporters, and who can tell us the hard truths we need to hear. When you work in an organisation, you typically have a team of people who will do that for you. When you step out into your own business, you need to find that team.

Lisa overcame her loneliness by working hard on reconnecting with those she had lost touch with (and some of these conversations needed apologies). She also worked out what support she needed, and reached out and got it.

She reviewed this on a quarterly basis to ensure she had the right people in her circle. (We will explore the need to create the right circle for you in Myth #12: "I have people around me and that's enough.)

The first step to connecting with people is to recognise what you're feeling. Is it loneliness, or is it something else? Are you truly making the effort to reach out?

Here are three tips that helped Lisa become less of a hermit:

1. **Get out more**

   Find and connect with like-minded individuals – in person. You need to find the people who share similar values to you, who you can count on, and who you can call when you've had a crappy day.

2. **Find your tribe**

   Lisa had been to a few networking events and had "clicked" with one or two people, but never found her "home". She had to reframe how she approached these events and keep trying. So, she made a deal with herself to go to one networking event a month. Eventually, her circle of friends and like-minded people grew, and she found her tribe.

3. **Love them hard**

   When you find your tribe, you automatically love them to pieces. That's how I feel now with my tribe. Did I find them all in the same place? I should be so lucky! But are they connected in some way? Yes, they are – to me!

There really is no need to feel lonely in business – all you need is the desire to go out, chat with people and genuinely connect. I know that, at times, this can feel scary, but once you do it a few times, you will become a pro!

Truth #5:

It takes a village (a carefully selected one)

The truth is, it still takes a village. Not just to raise a child, but to grow a business or raise your leadership level. You cannot do it on your own.

The most successful women know this. They identify who they need in their tribe and they intentionally bring them in. Not only do they bring them in, like any team, they swap them around to ensure they leverage their unique skills and experience in a way that makes sense.

Here are some words from one of my amazing clients, Melitta, who demonstrates this:

It Takes A Village

Leadership can be lonely. Even when you work for a really supportive company with a highly engaged and caring team, it can still be lonely.

Having had a very transient life, both in childhood and in my career (7 interstate moves, 12 new communities and 16 house moves), I've got forming new friends down to a fine art. I probably used to consider myself somewhat of an expert in turning strangers into friends. But the thing I really underestimated prior to joining Thriving Women was how critical it was to have a "tribe". A place where you belong. A place of deep trust where the care around you is matched by the level of challenge, because these people care deeply about the success of you as a human, as a professional, as a leader.

As I've developed through my leadership roles, I've found what makes the real difference is the people you have around you. I find leadership beyond a certain level of experience is less about new models, frameworks and knowing more stuff, and much more about reflection, holding a mirror up, and having a trusted few who can challenge you directly while caring deeply.

I have never felt more accelerated in my career, more productively challenged than now, and it can be attributed to my tribe. These women have cried with me, laughed with me, celebrated at every point with me. They are my cheer squad, my pit crew, and my butt kickers!

– Melitta

"I should be able to do it on my own."

Keep. Stop. Start.

After reading this chapter, think deeply and ask yourself:

What do I need to **KEEP** doing?

_____

_____

_____

What do I need to **STOP** doing?

_____

_____

_____

What do I need to **START** doing?

_____

_____

_____

Myth #6:

"I need to multitask to be successful."

Are we, as women, buying into the idea that we need to be superhuman? Do we create our own set of expectations that compound the issue instead of reassessing our priorities? Do we need to feel like we are in control, keeping all the plates spinning at home and work?

Have we fallen into the habit of multitasking? We do a quick check of Facebook while watching television or reading a book and suddenly lose 30 minutes. We constantly switch between tasks and expect each task to be completed well – but they rarely are. Does this sound familiar to you?

When we multitask, it's like having all of those tabs open on your internet browser, which makes the computer (or your brain, in this instance) slower.

So, why do we behave this way? According to reMarkable, every time we use iPads, smartphones and laptops, we get a hit of dopamine. We associate the hit of dopamine with the very act of multitasking, and the cycle continues.[22]

The truth is, it's impossible to be in control of all areas of our lives all the time. If we try to give 100% to everything, we end up burnt out. We feel disappointed in ourselves, as though we aren't giving 100% to anything.

Research suggests that multitasking can reduce our productivity by as much as 40%. It can also affect our happiness – but it depends on the length of time we spend multitasking. For instance, multitasking over a shorter period of time (10 minutes to one hour) tends to make people unhappy, but over the course of a day, it has the opposite effect. We enjoy variety, but having a number of things to do over a short period makes us discontent.[23]

So, why is multitasking detrimental? Research suggests:[24]

- Being focused on a few different things versus one thing at a time is not good for our brain.
- It pushes our brain to do too many things, when it has been designed to do one thing at a time.
- The quality of the work may end up being questionable.
- Our stress levels increase.
- We can't be creative when we are not focused on the task at hand.

When we multitask, we also tend to put ourselves last. We don't value ourselves or the value we bring as much as we should. In turn, this negatively impacts how others view us and even what we get paid.

Is there a better way? Could we make some better choices about where we spend our time, energy and attention? Could we ask for help? Are we brave enough? Or do we wear "busy" as a badge of honour? Do we think being busy means we are important?

Truth #6:

I need to ruthlessly prioritise to be successful

Your diary is a reflection of your values. If you do not prioritise the important, the urgent will take over, and you can trust in the fact there will always be something urgent, even if it is not important.

Success comes to those who prioritise – ruthlessly. The key to this is being accountable. The most successful women hold themselves accountable to someone: a mentor, coach, sponsor or even a tough but fair friend who doesn't buy into the excuses!

And what should your number-one priority be? You.

Are You Worth It?

When you multitask, and when you are always fighting other people's fires, the work that's important to you, your priorities and even your self-worth can come last.

Let me explain.

I don't think I have ever been called arrogant – well, not out loud, at least! One thing is for sure, I know my worth. When I entered into my business full time, I knew I was not the cheapest in my field. I knew I might be seen as expensive, but I also knew the right people would find me or I would find them. I made my worth a priority.

A potential client named Anne called me. She had been highly recommended to have a conversation with me about some career coaching. We talked about what an engagement would look like, what she wanted out of it, and what we thought we could do together. I didn't dillydally on price, I just put it out there and if she thought I was valuable and could help, we would do business. If she didn't, we wouldn't – no hard feelings.

I'd been talking to Anne about the type of women I'd coached. I'd helped them get paid what they were worth, doing jobs they loved. Anne was very excited. But towards the end of our chat, she asked me if I would discount my price because she felt I was too expensive. Boy, this was a challenging and ironic conversation. I had a choice to make: to play above the line or below the line.[25]

"I need to multitask to be successful."

Above the Line
Thinking & Behaviours

- Make choices
- See possibilities
- Solve
- Seek solutions
- Accountable
- Take action

- Take responsibility
- Find better ways
- Seek & provide feedback

- Hope
- See it
- Own it

Make a choice!

Things happen but it is your response that determines if the outcome is ultimately positive or negative

Below the Line
Thinking & Behaviours

- Victim
- Block
- Excuses

- Ignore
- Deny
- Blame
- Find fault

- Obstacles
- Do nothing
- No control
- See problems
- Wait for others
- See failure

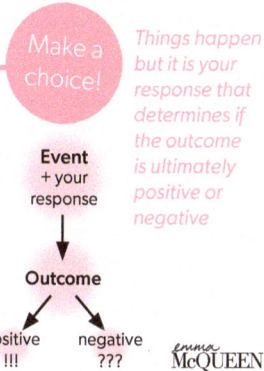

Event + your response

↓

Outcome

positive !!! negative ???

emma McQUEEN

Not one to shrink from a challenge, or an opportunity to use my courage in a subject I am passionate about, it will be no surprise to you that I chose to play above the line. I told Anne it didn't feel right for me to discount my price based on her perception. The irony of the fact that I had talked about women getting paid their worth yet Anne had asked me to lower my price was a little lost on her. You see, if you don't value yourself, if you don't make yourself a priority, no one else will.

Time and again, I see women accepting positions, career changes and salaries that are lower than what they are worth. According to the Australian Bureau of Statistics, even though the percentage of women in leadership roles has increased, pay equity still requires work, with the national gender pay gap sitting at 14%.[26]

The thing is, we, as women, *are doing it to ourselves.* Not all the time, not in every situation, but when we talk about "women supporting women", I don't think we mean, "My friend has a new business, so I will ask her for a discount." It should mean, "My friend has a new business, so I will pay full price *and* I will tell everyone I know about her new business *and* I will do whatever I can to support her." Am I right?

So, how does one start to step into their worth? Here's what I did in my situation with Anne:

1. **I chose to play above the line.** I refuse to play any other way. I was clear with Anne about what she was asking for and told her how I felt about it.

2. **I chose to see it as my issue.** I clearly had not demonstrated enough value to make it worthwhile for Anne, and in no way did I excuse myself from the conversation.

3. **I gave her some alternatives.** These were in the form of online courses, reading and other coaches to contact.

My point is, if you do not value yourself, no one else will. Why should they? Why should someone else value you if you do not value yourself? And if you don't value yourself, why? What can you do to lift your self-esteem, to push away those loud voices that tell you you're not worth it?

Here is where the rubber hits the road: there is only one person who can fix this, and it's you. You may need to get some help to come up with strategies to park that negative inner voice. I work with many women who struggle with this.

Do The Work!

In Myth #3: "It shouldn't be this hard," we discussed showing up (or the act of not showing up and what this can mean). A natural progression of this is to talk about doing the work, or GSD (Getting Shiz Done)!

When you are trying to multitask and you feel under the pump, it is so easy to feel overwhelmed and get bogged down in how much work there is to do. Instead of getting on with it, we sit on it and stress about how much there is to do. This is a trap we are all guilty of falling into, but one that we need to recognise and get out of immediately.

Take Bree, for example. Bree is a busy working mum, like many of us. She juggles kids, work, a busy household and (when she gets time) a life. Recently, it all got the better of her.

Bree had just taken on a new role at work, a role she was more than capable of. In fact, it was her dream role. However, the timing coincided with her partner being out of town for business, the start of a new school year for her eldest child, her youngest child getting sick, and her kids being unusually emotional (feeding off her vibes).

Her go-to feeling in this unusually stressful situation was that of absolute overwhelm. It left her paralysed. She had no ability to get on with it. Instead of doing the work and taking small steps forward, she let everything go. This resulted in her boss pulling her aside to question whether she was keeping up with the changed workload.

Not Getting Shiz Done can be due to many reasons. We all find ourselves in situations where we are overwhelmed, suffering mind blocks, lacking confidence. At these times, we need to acknowledge it and implement a strategy to ensure we can get on with it. One thing I find helpful is taking the time (when I am not stressed) to develop a self-care plan that I can access when I am feeling overwhelmed. Use the following template to work out your self-care plan.[27]

"I need to multitask to be successful."

Self-Care Plan

Professional
1.

2.

3.

Physical
1.

2.

3.

Psychological
1.

2.

3.

Emotional
1.

2.

3.

Spiritual
1.

2.

3.

Relational
1.

2.

3.

Similar to not showing up, not Getting Shiz Done can have many ongoing negative impacts:

- The work compounds.
- People notice you – for the wrong reasons.
- You get a bad reputation.

One of my core values in life is progress over perfection. This is all about not sweating the small stuff and just getting on with things. It's about not being scared to give things a go. It's about trusting in yourself that you are capable. Sounds simple in theory, and it is quite simple in practice, too.

So, how do we get on with it and Get Shiz Done? Here is my simple yet effective advice:

- **Write a list of ONLY three things**

  I write a list of only three things to get done in a day. I prioritise this list. Of course, I have a longer list, but if I get those three things done, I feel like I have achieved what I need to. If you need it, keep a longer list somewhere else.

  Writing down the tasks you need to complete and prioritising them is so simple, yet super effective. Think of all those things that pop into your head daily, the things you continually put to the back of your mind but which are important to complete. Write them down so you can focus on actually completing them. The bonus is the absolute sense of achievement you get from ticking items off the list.

- **Stop procrastinating – do the HARDEST thing first!**

  I do the hardest thing on my list first, then give myself a fist pump for getting it done!

- **Stop distractions and focus**

  Distractions are all around us and can be difficult to avoid. However, you do have some control over this. Switch off your email notifications, put your phone in do-not-disturb mode, block out your calendar and request no disruptions from work colleagues for set times during the day. Use this time to focus on nothing else but the tasks on your to-do list. Eliminating all other distractions will make the task at hand so much simpler. You may even find you complete it quicker than you thought you would.

- **Seek an accountability buddy**

  Sometimes, not being accountable to anyone means we don't do the work (this is something I see a lot with small business owners). Find someone you can share your goals with and check in with them regularly. Being accountable to someone other than yourself will help keep you on track.

- **Revisit your goals**

  I like to set goals yearly, monthly and weekly. Monitoring these goals is critical to ensuring you are on track to reach them. If you are not Getting Shiz Done, chances are, you are not going to achieve your goals. Take time to reflect on your goals and put strategies in place to ensure you are on track to see results.

Implementing these strategies will set you on the right path to Getting Shiz Done. Just think how good you will feel when you tick off those items on your to-do list, knowing you are on top of your workload and where you need to be to move forward.

Oh, and don't forget to treat yourself when you feel like you have been super effective. This could be as simple as going for a walk or getting a coffee – something to let yourself know, "I did good!"

The Power Of NO

Do you ever have the feeling things are getting out of control? Do you find yourself saying yes to everything – yes to friends, yes to family, yes to work (especially work you don't love)?

When we constantly say yes, we also say no – to ourselves. Saying yes all the time makes it difficult to have clarity and focus on our goals. We end up doing too much multitasking, focusing on the urgent and not prioritising the important.

Let me ask you this: *What have you said yes to when you should have said no?* This is something we are all guilty of doing. As a business owner, leader or employee, what happens when you say yes to work you don't want to do? Don't get me wrong, sometimes we have to suck it up and get a job we don't love done. What I'm talking about is work that doesn't align with your values or purpose, work that is uninspiring and deflating.

The reasons why we feel compelled to say yes vary from person to person. It may be because we don't have clarity and focus on our priorities to begin with. Whatever our reason for saying yes, we all need to learn the power of saying no. If we are not actively saying no, then we are saying yes – at least, that's what others will assume. A non-answer is an answer, unfortunately.

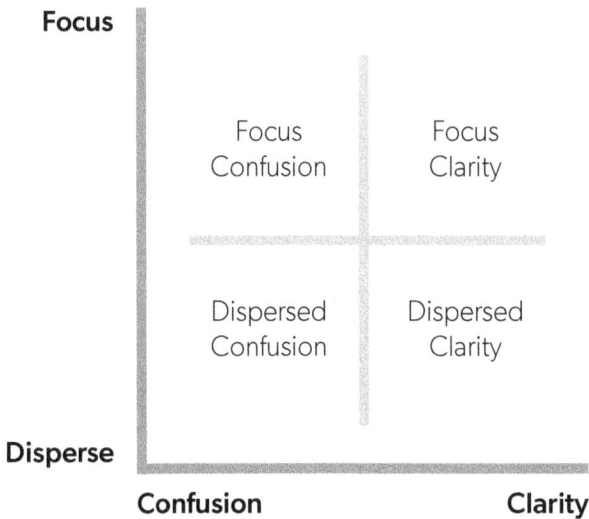

Focus

Focus Confusion	Focus Clarity
Dispersed Confusion	Dispersed Clarity

Disperse

Confusion   **Clarity**

Let me tell you about Kaylee. Kaylee started her own business out of an opportunity she felt too good to pass up. The problem was that while she had a vague idea of the services she would offer clients, she didn't have clarity surrounding this idea. As a result, she said yes to any job opportunity presented to her and was constantly multitasking. This led to her having too many things to focus on with no one real focus, causing her a ridiculous sense of overwhelm.

We chatted and were able to get some clarity around her passion and purpose. She was then focused and able to say no to the work that didn't align with her goals and priorities, which meant she no longer felt overwhelmed.

We've talked about overwhelm and how it can be an incredibly unproductive emotion. It causes us to be scattered, unfocused and paralysed. Having clarity and focus assists in ensuring you can relieve yourself of overwhelm and focus on more positive emotions.

So, how do we go about saying no?

I remind myself that if I say yes to something, it means I am saying no to something else by default, so I need to be sure the thing I say yes to is something I truly want to do.

I also listen to my intuition. If your gut says no, you need to pay attention to it. If it says no and then you say yes, you will feel out of alignment. This can manifest in a physical sense – e.g. feeling sick, headache, tiredness.

Because women generally like to be people-pleasers, we tend to default to yes. I believe people don't mind it when you say no if they understand the reasoning behind it (for those in small business, you may not need to give a reason, but for those in organisations, this may be a little trickier). When it is a definite "NO", explain why: "I can't take on this piece of work right now because I am at capacity; however, I can refer you to…"

Keep in mind that saying no isn't about *not* being nice – it's about setting boundaries for yourself and others.

If you're not sure how to get started saying no, try this:

SAY NO CHALLENGE

Wanna Say No To Something?

Here's how it works. For one week, pick something each day you wouldn't usually say no to. Instead of automatically saying yes to it, say NO instead.

It doesn't have to be something terribly important. In fact, it's better if it's not while you get into the rhythm of saying no. It just needs to be something others would normally take for granted.

For example, if you're shopping with the kids and they always ask for ice cream, and you'd rather not buy it, but you usually do because it's easier than fighting over it – don't! Say NO and don't back down. The trick here is to avoid the nagging. If they keep asking (chances are, this will happen if they are used to getting a yes), drop down to their eye level and say, "You have already asked and I have answered you, the answer is no." Do this with a smile on your face, so they know you are not angry but you are serious. Repeat this phrase each time they ask.

Another example is when a telemarketer calls and you don't want to hurt their feelings. How often do you let them finish their spiel and either set an appointment you don't intend to keep or engage them in conversation? Let's not do this. Politely tell them you don't have any interest right now, thank them for their time, hang up and get on with your day.

Keep a record of how you feel when you say no during this week. Do you feel differently about saying no at the end of the week? If you don't, consider doing the exercise for a longer time period.

Strive to say no without feeling guilty. Recognise that you have a right to say no whenever you wish, and to feel good about doing so.

"I need to multitask to be successful."

Keep. Stop. Start.

After reading this chapter, think deeply and ask yourself:

What do I need to **KEEP** doing?

_____

_____

_____

What do I need to **STOP** doing?

_____

_____

_____

What do I need to **START** doing?

_____

_____

_____

Myth #7:

"Our inner voice holds us back."

We all have that inner voice, male *and* female. It's an internal dialogue and a well-integrated pattern of self-destructive thoughts.

You might have several inner critics: the self-doubter, the martyr, the know-it-all, the judge and the wimpy kid with a diary. No matter how many or how loud those voices are, every person has them.

The issue we need to get on top of is how to listen to and manage our relationship with our doubts. It sits on your shoulder and tells you that you can't, you're not good enough, you wonder if you can pull this off, you wonder if you will fail – actually, you wonder when you will fail, not if. You wonder when people will find out you know absolutely nothing, you wonder if you have the energy to keep going, how you will meet everyone's expectations and needs and have some room left for yourself. The list goes on.

As a leader or small business owner, you wonder if you are as good as your heart believes you are, while that inner voice asks you what on earth you are thinking. You feel nervous because deep down, you wonder if you can make enough money to "be a success".

The inner critic loves to hold on to the beliefs that may have been true years ago, but are now difficult to shake and have almost become habitual – a safety net, if you will. Safe because the inner critic convinces us these beliefs are there to protect us, not strangle us.

That inner voice means you alternate between confidence and self-doubt, getting on with it and paralysis. You continually ask yourself, "What if I fail?"

But what if you don't? *What if you don't?*

Is your inner voice holding you back?

Truth #7:

You can choose which voice you listen to

Managing your mindset is the most important thing. If you don't manage it, you leave your thoughts up to chance – and, chances are, negative thoughts will start to creep in.

Think of it as like putting healthy food into your body. When you nourish your body with nutritious food, you feel energised and ready to tackle anything. If you eat too many unhealthy foods, you feel sluggish and unwell.

It's the same with your mindset. If you don't nurture it and keep it in check, everything can seem too hard, and you struggle to reach your goals.

You have a choice. You can choose which voice you listen to, and it can radically alter your mindset, which can dramatically change how you behave and the results you get. It's called "observer-created reality". Your mindset influences your behaviours, which affect your results.

You can take back control. The first step is to notice your inner critics and observe how they play out. The most successful women are attuned to their inner critics, and they bring their tribe in to listen and challenge them. One of the ways to take back control is to "catch" the inner critic and challenge it. Easier said than done, I know. Here's what it looks like…

Jenny puts her hand up for a promotion. Jenny's inner critic thinks, "My accomplishments are all flukes, I am just lucky." Jenny stops and asks her critic if this is true and reframes her brain by saying aloud some of her most recent achievements and how hard she had worked for them.

Call Out That Inner Critic

Melissa came to me because she was concerned about her confidence. When we unpacked this concern, we discovered the real issue was her inner critic.

Melissa struggled with the imposter syndrome. It drove her thoughts, telling her she wasn't good enough, she wasn't up to it, she was going to make a mistake, she was going to fail, she wasn't going to get the promotion… the list went on.

Her poor brain was so full of these hurtful comments that we needed to do something to turn her mindset around.

Fact Or Fiction?

Melissa and I worked hard to identify the negative thoughts as they came to her. We captured them and inspected them. As soon as a negative thought landed in her brain, she would take a moment to pause and check in to see whether the thought had any factual relevance. She would thoroughly inspect it to see if it was fact or fiction.

During this process, Melissa asked herself some questions. These are simple questions you can ask yourself, too, to make sure your negative voice isn't the only voice you hear:

- Is what I'm thinking factual?
- Where is the evidence?
- How do I objectively know I am a failure in this or that I don't have what it takes to complete this task?

Once you've asked yourself these questions, you can work out whether that negative voice is based in reality. I think you'll find that, most of the time, it's not.

Reframe Your Brain

Now you know there's no evidence to support your negative voice, you can reframe your brain. Yes, you *can* change your negative inner commentary so it is helpful!

For instance, if you're about to take on a job or task you haven't performed before, and your critical voice tells you that you can't do it, ask yourself, "Why can't I do it? Where are the facts?"

This allows you to reframe that inner voice: "I'm learning something new; therefore, it's not about *not* being able to do it – I just haven't been given the chance yet. There's no evidence to say I can't do it. In fact, there's every chance I will succeed."

It's A Daily Process

Overcoming the imposter syndrome is not always easy. It's something many of us face and must work on daily. Unfortunately, for women, it's there in the background all the time. It seems to be a little kinder to men – or perhaps they don't pay quite as much attention to it as women.

One thing for sure is that we must all consciously and continuously work on managing our mindset.

I like to think that mindset, mojo and motivation go together. When all three elements are aligned, success is imminent.

Keep. Stop. Start.

After reading this chapter, think deeply and ask yourself:

What do I need to **KEEP** doing?

_____

_____

_____

What do I need to **STOP** doing?

_____

_____

_____

What do I need to **START** doing?

_____

_____

_____

emma McQUEEN

Myth #8:

"I just need to tick things off the list."

In today's hyper-connected world of instant gratification, the ability to think deeply is becoming scarce. People now experience a meeting cancellation with the same relief as the previous generation did with a two-week vacation.

We are jam-packed, booked up and stressed out. It does not work. You can get things done, or you can be productive. You can create a feeling of productivity, or you can do the work that gets results.

I am the first to admit, I love a good to-do list, but really, what the heck for? To make us feel guilty about all the shiz we didn't quite get done? To make us feel like we are not good enough? We have to-do lists on our phone, our computer, our watch, our fridge... it's endless.

Technology can be used to help us be productive or it can be the devil (those of you who have children will know just how that devil shows up!). Are we using our technology to our advantage or are we beholden to it?

> *"When you are writing your TO-DO list, don't forget your TO-BE list."*
>
> Emma McQueen

Truth #8:

You need laser focus, and clarity gets focus

While it is comforting to believe you'll be successful if you keep ticking actions or items off the to-do list, be careful not to get lulled into a false sense of progress.

Having clarity means the distractions disappear. You don't focus on the shiny new objects anymore, you just get in and do the work. You take small steps forward (and some steps back, let's be honest), but you keep your eyes up and you do the work.

Remember to celebrate the small successes along the way. Each little success adds up. The most successful women know this as they prioritise clarity. They create space for clarity. And most of all, they protect their most precious commodity: time.

"Clarity is like focusing a strong source of light on your goal to make it more visible. With a clarity of purpose comes acceptance of the mission and the job at hand."

McWinner Yawman

A Love/Hate Relationship With Technology

A typical night in any household: the kids get picked up from school, homework is completed and dinner is eaten. After dinner, everyone flops on the couch in front of the TV. But no one is really watching TV. Everyone is sitting around, playing on their smartphone or tablet, checking out who's doing what on social media or looking up information on the net.

It's a far cry from the "olden" days, when a family had no option but to sit around, listening to the wireless and discussing their day with each other. If you wanted to find out what someone was doing, you'd pick up the phone and chat. If you wanted information about the world, you'd pick up a newspaper or book. Now, Wikipedia is more commonly used than an encyclopaedia!

This is why I have a love/hate relationship with technology. I love how easy it is to have any information I want at my fingertips, but I hate the fact that we are becoming "zombies".

Our kids no longer seem to go outside to play or nag us to use the home phone (I know some people who no longer even have a home phone!). They are either preoccupied with video games or using their smartphone or tablet to connect with those around them.

Where do our kids learn this behaviour?

- From their mates who do the same thing.
- From us – we are always "on".
- The fact that life seems so busy – we never have downtime.
- The fact we don't often go outside to play a family game, go for a walk or enjoy the sunshine.

Answer this question: "Where's your phone right now?" Is it beside you, in your bag but you regularly check it, or perhaps even in your hand? How often does it distract you from the work or activity you should be doing, eating into your time and eroding your clarity?

Smartphones and other technology are essential to the way we communicate in our businesses and daily lives. However, excessive use can put us back into that trap of always being "busy" but not productive. It corrodes that laser focus we need to achieve our goals and get results – not to mention our relationships.

A recent study[28] on smartphone usage conducted by Deakin University found:

- 40% of people surveyed felt lost without their phone.
- 34% lost sleep due to the time spent on their phone.
- 54% found themselves occupied on their phone when they should be doing other things, causing problems.

Dr Sharon Horwood, a lead researcher and psychology lecturer at Deakin University, says: "We can think of problematic smartphone use as someone who has started to use their phone compulsively and where that compulsive use has started to impact on their daily functioning. That could be their productivity, social relationships, physical health, or emotional well-being."

Dr Horwood says that given 88% of Australians have smartphones, we must feel as though we are getting something good from them, but excessive use can result in a low mood, reduced physical fitness, sleep deprivation, and reduced academic performance.

To try to balance out our use of technology, my husband and I have started to leave our phones at home when we go out for a meal with our family. When we do go out and I look around, I have found it amazing to see how many people are on their phones, not talking to each other. It's sad but something we all seem to do these days.

We have also made another rule in our house: technology does not rule us! This can be hard to manage some days, as we are a blended family and we do need to communicate across two different households. But at the end of the day, when we are all sitting down together and talking, it's well worth having the rule that no distractions are allowed.

We also turn off all technology during dinner and have a focused conversation as a family. We go around the table and each talk about three things: the best part of our day, one thing we are grateful for and something we did that was kind for another person. This is easily the best part of my day.

So tonight, when you get home, try saying to your family "NO TECHNOLOGY". Sure, you may meet some objections at first, but start small (maybe one hour and build up from there) so you can sit around your table after dinner and connect, interact and talk about your day.

Having said that, I have to admit (and please don't tell the kids) that the amount of knowledge children have about technology is amazing. I'm only a Gen X, yet whenever I need to know how to do anything "techy", my teenagers are on hand to show me. I guess it's what they are growing up with, so I may as well embrace the knowledge they can share.

Here are some helpful tips from Dr Horwood on healthy smartphone use:

• Turn off all non-essential notifications, so your phone doesn't constantly interrupt you.

- Set aside a block of time per day to look at your social media feeds, if that's what typically distracts you.

- Use the screen time functions on your phone to set limits on daily phone use.

- To improve your sleep quality, don't keep your phone beside your bed at night. Preferably, charge it in a different room.

- If you find your socialising is restricted to your smartphone, aim to build daily interactions with people in real life.

- Try to get up and move more throughout the day to reduce sedentary behaviour and improve your mental wellbeing.

Keep. Stop. Start.

After reading this chapter, think deeply and ask yourself:

What do I need to **KEEP** doing?

_____

_____

_____

What do I need to **STOP** doing?

_____

_____

_____

What do I need to **START** doing?

_____

_____

_____

Myth #9:

"I'll fake it till I make it."

Almost every person at some point has been told to fake it till they make it. The problem is, it doesn't work.

The number of times I have heard this phrase – and even said it myself earlier in my career – astounds me. We use the phrase as a way to say, "I'm not confident that I can do this," or, "My self-worth won't let me own that I can do this." It's used as a phrase of deflection.

So, what does the saying "fake it till you make it" actually mean? Wikipedia suggests that "by imitating confidence, competence, and an optimistic mindset, a person can realise those qualities in their real life."[29]

People often mistake "faking it" for confidence. For example, if you are more shy than extroverted and need to expand your network for your business to grow, you do what "confident" people do: you show up to a networking event and find the least intense person to strike up a conversation with. Faking it doesn't work. The truth is, faking it only works when you identify something within yourself that's holding you back.

When we fake it, we pretend. We hope that by pretending, eventually, we will feel confident – so confident, in fact, that we trick our brain into thinking it works!

When you pretend, you are the very essence of being fake, not authentic or at all true to yourself.

Truth #9:

Confidence gets belief

When you change your behaviour, the feeling follows. As you begin to focus on the right activity, you have small wins along the way, and you start to feel a little more confident.

For example, have you ever started going to the gym with a personal trainer and had no idea how to use the equipment, let alone the belief that you could do it and get fit?

Let's explore this idea using the confidence model:

The Confidence Model

In the beginning, all you need is the **discipline** to get out the door and head to the gym. Then you need **consistency** to create a **habit**. When you have been going to the gym for a while, you understand what you need to do. You have the **experience** to do what you need to do, and the more you do it, the more you increase your **confidence**.

It's the same when it comes to leadership and running your own business.

Consistency Builds Credibility

I get asked for advice and to speak at events regularly, and one of the things I am often asked about is how do I find the time to write in a disciplined way. Writing has not always been a priority for me, but I do have the gift of discipline, and I believe that consistency in everything you do enables credibility.

Consistency doesn't just happen. You need to sit down and consciously plan it. Consistency can be anything from having a follow-up plan to calling people instead of emailing them, to having templates to help you write regularly.

Company strategist Eric Holtzclaw gives five reasons why leaders and business owners need to be consistent:[30]

1. Consistency allows for measurement.
2. It creates accountability.
3. It establishes your reputation.
4. It makes you relevant.
5. It maintains your message.

I agree. When you are inconsistent, people find it difficult to trust you. They don't want to work with you because they don't know what to expect from you.

Here are four things you can do to become consistent:

1. Non-negotiables

Choose the things that are not negotiable from a consistency perspective. For me, it's paying attention to the numbers, regular business development, writing each week, and conducting professional, respectful follow-up using the phone (versus email).

2. Allocate time

Everything in business takes time, doesn't it? I can guarantee that if it's not in the calendar, it won't happen, so I allocate the amount of time I think a task will take in my diary. This means the next step is probably the most important.

3. Keep the appointment with yourself

How often do we forgo that time with ourselves because something "urgent" or "more important" has come up? It can be hard to keep that appointment with yourself, but it's well worth it.

4. Do the work

Do the work to set yourself up for success in the long term. How you like to work also determines how much you can achieve. I like to work using the Pomodoro technique (25-minute intervals separated by 5-minute breaks, as previously discussed). I also review my work to ensure I am happy with it before continuing.

What about you? Have you tried to be consistent and achieved success? Or are you one of many who struggle with this? By following the steps above, by working steadily and consistently, you will build your experience and the habits needed to achieve success, and your confidence will naturally bloom and grow – no faking it required!

Keep. Stop. Start.

After reading this chapter, think deeply and ask yourself:

What do I need to **KEEP** doing?

_____

_____

_____

What do I need to **STOP** doing?

_____

_____

_____

What do I need to **START** doing?

_____

_____

_____

Myth #10:

"Motivation is the key."

Why is it that Monday is the most common day to start a diet, or the 1st of January to kickstart resolutions, or the 1st of the month to start a campaign?

We wait for the calendar or the motivation to get started. The truth is, motivation might get you started, but habits are what keep you going.

In his book, *Atomic Habits*, James Clear talks about the fact we sometimes dismiss the small changes we make because they don't seem to matter much at any given point in time. But we do know that all these small habits add up, and they can be the difference between achieving success and it forever being out of reach.

Habits, rather than motivation, are not just important for career and business success. They're critical to a happy personal life, too.

When The Strength Of Motivation Goes Wrong

Jen had been in her own business for just over two years. She was enjoying it, getting excellent results, had been nominated for some awards and was trailblazing in her space. When I asked her why she thought she needed my help, Jen told me she didn't think the results were enough, that the work she put in far outweighed the results she was getting.

Typically, when people come to me, they think they are dealing with one particular issue. But scratch the surface and the real need pops out. In Jen's case, it was a serious issue of zero balance. She was so engaged in her work that she had allowed her relationships to falter: her hubby and kids felt like they only got the "end-of-the-day bits" of her, and she did not catch up with her friends anymore. Jen felt bored if she wasn't talking about business, but she knew she was the one who was boring *because* she only wanted to talk about work.

Jen's issue had nothing to do with results. What it came down to was the work itself was so satisfying to Jen, she had wrapped her self-worth around it, to the point that when she wasn't working, she felt guilty, as if she was losing time. She always felt like she should be doing more. Her brain wasn't letting her rest for a second.

Jen was achieving massive results in her business, but she had no life outside of it. The habits she had formed were incredibly damaging to her and those around her. She was not sleeping or eating well, and she was working way too many hours. Her family was deeply unhappy. She knew something needed to change, but she didn't want it to be at the expense of her success (or how she saw success).

It's ironic that I get to serve these types of clients. Do you know why? Because this was me when I started my business. I was so passionate about it, there was so much to do, yet it was so unsatisfying. When there is no balance in your life, it can all turn to crap so quickly.

I was well placed to help Jen out!

Truth #10:

Commitment gets action

Creating a habit can be hard work. No doubt you have heard that it takes 21 days to develop a habit (although it isn't quite that clear-cut[31]), and there are many hacks to help you create them.

I prefer to think of good habits as an unwavering commitment to the work you do. You are clear on what needs to get done, you have routines or systems in place, and you just get the work done – the "right" work, the work that will push you further to your end goal. You don't rely on motivation, which comes and goes. Instead, you commit every day to your goal, and you take the action that will get you there.

Successful women know that taking the right action every day will inch them closer to their end goal, and they are relentless in their dedication to achieving this.

Let's go back to my client Jen.

Jen worked hard to create a practical plan that would work for her. I have to say (and she would be fine with me saying it), Jen was very unhappy with the plan, but she understood the common sense behind it. She knew something drastic had to change, and I was able to demonstrate the benefits of changing her lifestyle and creating new habits. What this turnaround took, though, was Jen's blind faith in me – especially at the start.

Firstly, Jen analysed a week in the life of her business and was able to identify how many hours she worked, what she spent her time on, and how her energy felt throughout the day. To Jen's surprise, she was constantly putting in 16-hour days. That's 16 hours out of 24 hours every day, Monday to Sunday! Wowsers!

I have seen some clients pull these hours – usually for a project or a limited amount of time. After that time, they get their life back. To always be switched on with no finish line in sight is unsustainable. Jen didn't realise she was doing damage to herself by working these hours.

What's more, working these long hours isn't productive. A Stanford research paper found that people who worked 70 hours per week didn't actually get more work done than their peers who worked 56 hours.[32]

So, we put some simple steps in place to help Jen:

1. We agreed to the outcomes and how we would measure them.
2. We made a 30-, 60- and 90-day plan.
3. Jen spoke to the key people in her life.

The outcome we wanted at the end of the 90 days was for Jen to be working 6–8 hours a day. This would give her family the "good bits" of her and not the leftover pieces. It would also allow her time with friends and for her success to continue.

We also had to work on Jen's mindset regarding what success looked like for her.

We made a plan. We broke that plan into 30-day segments to make the transition a little easier and to ensure Jen could commit to each item.

In the first 30 days:

- Jen spoke to her family about her 90-day plan, acknowledging that things needed to change and she was keen to make it work, but also that she would need help to stick to the plan.

- They committed to helping her and she committed to not beating herself up if she slipped up for a day.

- Jen agreed to stop working 16 hours a day and start working towards 8 (ouch, I know!), rather than go cold turkey on this. She left her office at 5pm every day, closed the door, announced to her family she was "home" and she was not allowed to head back into the office.

- Jen booked the important things in her calendar and began to stick to the appointments she created for herself.

- We outsourced. We found Jen a virtual assistant to manage her calendar, a bookkeeper to manage the invoicing and a cleaner to maintain her house.

- Jen went to the doctor and had some tests to ensure the stress hadn't done any permanent damage to her body.

The results:

1. Jen had withdrawals from working so much. On the one hand, she knew cutting back was going to be beneficial to everyone around her, but on the flip side, she felt "lazy" for not working the kind of hours she had.

2. She slept better – not immediately, but after about week two. She told me because she was switching off so early (read: she was a bit bored), she had well and truly wound down by bedtime.

3. She was present with her family. They had taken to playing card games after dinner and this family time made everything else seem easier.

---

*"Habits are not a finish line to be crossed,
they are a lifestyle to be lived."*

James Clear

In the second 30 days:

- Jen did another analysis of her diary to check her progress. By outsourcing her calendar and invoicing, she had regained approximately 10–12 hours a week.

- She continued with the same activities from the first 30 days of her plan.

- Jen looked for more tasks to outsource. She found that once her calendar was sorted out (some tidying needed to happen first), the virtual assistant could take on other tasks, such as certain kinds of email, so she outsourced that, too.

- She began to allocate time in her calendar to socialise. We slotted in a two-hour window once a week so she could catch up with a friend.

The results:

1. Jen was focused before we began working together, but she learnt that taking breaks enabled her to think

more clearly and she used her time exceptionally well in smaller spurts.

2. She used some of her hours managing her virtual assistant, but she was also able to put systems in place to make things easier for both of them.

3. She was happy her relationships with her friends were being prioritised.

In the final 30 days:

- Jen embedded all the things from the first 60 days. We talked about what was working and kept those things, and got rid of what wasn't.

- She used pockets of time better (e.g. instead of listening to the radio in the car, she would call a client or listen to a podcast).

- She asked her family for feedback on how they thought her plan was working and if they had any suggestions.

The results:

1. Changing habits after several years is not the easiest thing to do, but the benefits certainly outweighed the pain for Jen. She was extremely disciplined once she was clear on how to make this work for her.

2. Jen's family has seen a massive change in her. She is more present with them and her relationships positively shifted in three short months.

3. She carves time out of her diary to manage her energy, changing this up with running, meditation and walking. She puts these activities in her diary and keeps the appointments with herself.

The verdict:

Having zero balance is not fun. We all know it; we just need a plan to make some healthy lifestyle choices and ensure we don't fall back into old habits. Once Jen was clear on what she needed, what she would not negotiate on and what needed to change, the change itself wasn't difficult.

Keep. Stop. Start.

After reading this chapter, think deeply and ask yourself:

What do I need to **KEEP** doing?

_____

_____

_____

What do I need to **STOP** doing?

_____

_____

_____

What do I need to **START** doing?

_____

_____

_____

Myth #11:

"All action leads to results."

We often think if we just keep moving, we will get results. "If I keep doing stuff, the results will follow."

Really? How long is that to-do list you have carried with you for the past five years?

Busyness does not get results. The *quality* of your to-do list is a better indicator of the results that will follow – not the number of things on there. If you are not getting the results you want, it's probably an indication of the quality of your to-do list.

I talk with a lot of my clients about just getting on and "doing the activity" that will move them forward. For many, that works, but the reality is that action sometimes leads to more action. It's like emails – the more you send, the more you receive, right?

Action leads to activity. Quality action leads to quality results.

Truth #11:

Clarity, Commitment, Confidence = Results

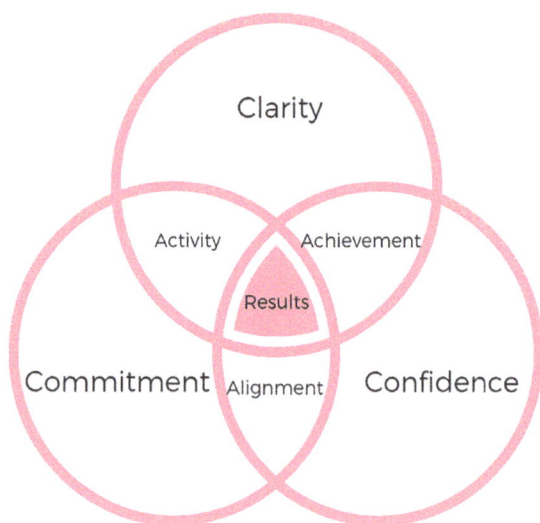

The truth is, a woman without a plan is, well, lost. You want to get clear on your priorities and quickly. The longer you stay in chaos, the harder it is to get out.

Clarity: we all crave it. It propels us forward. There is so much to do when you have your own business or team, isn't there?

Without clarity, though, it all makes zero sense. Getting clear on your priorities will help you remain focused. It will enable you to do the activity that needs to be done. When you commit to that activity, and when you do more of the *right* activity, you start to feel the momentum shift. You begin to feel small snippets of success and you start to feel confident.

You are no longer just busy. You are focused on the right kind of activities that will get you results.

The successful, go-getter woman knows exactly where she is headed. She may not know the "how" yet, but she will, and if she keeps focused on the "where", she will get there.

I was in a conversation with Evelyn. She was lamenting the fact she was not given the same opportunities as her colleagues. I asked what she was doing to find and secure those opportunities, and then I heard the words that made me cringe: "My results speak for themselves."

She is not alone in thinking this.

I wish the work did speak for itself, but results alone don't cut it anymore. You can't expect a promotion just on the results you currently get. When you go for a promotion, it's a step up, a chance to play more strategically, to think more globally. It's an opportunity to get results *through others*, to showcase your staff and help them think bigger.

Many women believe by talking about their achievements, they are gloating, or by showcasing their experience, they are bragging. But not talking about their accomplishments holds them back.

Are you worth it? Of course you are! And it's time to share it with the world. How do you go about taking control of your career and promotions? Here are a few steps I gave to Evelyn:

- **Work on the mindset**

  If you have a fixed mindset and feel like you can't do this, then you won't do it, simple. It's time to reframe this mindset and positively talk to yourself, then express that. Do you know the value you bring to your organisation and can you articulate it? Do you know how to communicate the value of what you do (not just the task) to others? If you win, who else around you wins? Your boss, your team, your organisation? Spread the word (and, if that makes you uncomfortable, try with a smaller win first).

- **Know the wins**

  To talk about the wins, you need to know what they are. Do you know? Do you reflect regularly enough to recognise your wins and the value they bring to your team, department or organisation?

- **Practise the pitch**

  No doubt you have heard of an elevator pitch. Does anyone ever pitch in an elevator? No, but it's always good to be ready! The same goes in this situation. Have your accomplishments ready to whip out when you need to – you never know when someone will ask you about your work, latest project or most recent results. Having a pitch and rehearsing it so it's authentic will help you get comfortable with it.

So, the next time you find yourself thinking, "My results speak for themselves," reframe it and say to yourself, "My results are excellent and I will show people my value by talking about the results I have achieved."

I know this might be hard for some of you, but you know what? You've got this!

Keep. Stop. Start.

After reading this chapter, think deeply and ask yourself:

What do I need to **KEEP** doing?

_____

_____

_____

What do I need to **STOP** doing?

_____

_____

_____

What do I need to **START** doing?

_____

_____

_____

Myth #12:

"I have people around me and that's enough."

In Myth #5: "I should be able to do it on my own," we looked at the importance of having a tribe. In this final myth, we explore the difference between having support and having the *right* support.

One of the biggest mistakes women in business and leadership make is that they don't have the right people around them. Having supportive leaders, partners or friends is great for social morale and emotional support, but how many of them call you on your critics, your excuses and your mindset?

You need a tribe that has your back, even if what they say is tough to hear. You need a cheer squad, a sponsor, a backer, a challenger, someone to hold up the mirror and, most of all, someone who raises the bar. Do you have these people?

Truth #12:

You need the right people around you

Every single person who is crafting a better life for themselves has their own reasons for doing so. They have their personal goals in life and their own way of getting there.

We are all as unique as our fingerprints. But one thing we all have in common is that we need the right tribe – honest people who will cheer us, support us, commiserate with us and give us constructive criticism. The people we can look at and say, "These are my people."

It's your journey, and no successful person ever did it alone. Who's got your back?

Who's In Your Circle?

I ran a workshop called, "Who's in your circle?" It was a useful workshop with reliable evidence behind it and research from the likes of Jim Collins[33] and Janine Garner.[34]

The session was thought-provoking and challenging. We talked specifically about two things: who the participants had in their circle, and who they needed in their circle. It had everyone thinking, which made me wonder: how many people don't think about who is in their space?

Have you heard the saying, *"The five people you hang out with, you become like"*?

Which five people do you hang out with the most? Are they the right people?

Many of us simply survive the day, doing the juggle in one way or another: children, older parents, family, marriages, you name it. I hear the groans in the room when I ask people to think about who's in their space – it's yet another thing "to do".

Here's the thing, though – if you don't take the time to think about who is in your circle, there are implications. You might not get that promotion you want, you might not get that new job, your business might not thrive. Surrounding yourself with the right people can be the difference between mere survival and success.

So, how do you take stock of who is in your circle to make sure it works for you? Follow this five-step process:

1. Analyse your current circle

Before you can start building your circle, you need to work out who is in it.

2. Look at who is in your existing network

Who is in your network now? Make some choices about whether they should stay or go. In Janine Garner's book, *It's Who You Know*,[35] she references the 12 types of people you do not want in your network (think saboteur and back-stabber). You need to make some decisions about the best people to have in your network for the goals you want to achieve. Do you need someone who will kick your butt, cheer you on, educate you about something? This means making the difficult choice to step back from some relationships while you lean into others.

3. Understand where the gaps are

You may have people in your circle who have always been there, and you may have people who are new to it. You may only have men in your circle, or you may only have women. Do a deep dive into your list and work out who knows each other, who doesn't, and whether you have enough people. Will a diverse mix of opinions help you grow?

4. Decide what you are prepared to give

Give first *always*. Choose how you will show up and make it mutually beneficial. This will be different for each person.

I can't stand the vague question, "Can I pick your brain?" What I do love, though, is when someone reaches out and is specific about their need – they have thought about it and have some well-considered questions. Give generously to the people in your circle, and they will give to you.

5. Get a move on

Sometimes, this process can feel overwhelming. The key is to keep moving and make sure you stay focused on who you need right now.

We could put it down to "luck" if we have a great circle, but I can say for sure there is no such thing as luck when cultivating the right circle for you. It's all about concerted effort, being clear on what you need and continuing to provide value to those around you.

Keep. Stop. Start.

After reading this chapter, think deeply and ask yourself:

What do I need to **KEEP** doing?

_____

_____

_____

What do I need to **STOP** doing?

_____

_____

_____

What do I need to **START** doing?

_____

_____

_____

emma
McQUEEN

I AM A GO GETTER

I KNOW THAT **PROGRESS GOES** AHEAD OF **PERFECTION**

I TRY THINGS,
NEW

FAIL FAST,

Get Back Up And Take To

//////////////////////// **HEART** ////////////////////////

WHAT I HAVE LEARNT. I CHOOSE

FULFILLMENT AND FREEDOM,

WHERE MY

PASSION MEET.
AND PURPOSE
I DO WORK I LOVE WITH **PEOPLE** I LIKE AND GET PAID MY WORTH.

I AM UNDEFINED ACTION, BUSYNESS WITHOUT RESULTS,
FREE THEORY OVER **PRACTICALITY**. MY BUSINESS GROWS
AS I TRY INNOVATIVE APPROACHES AND STEP
FROM FORWARD WITHOUT ALL THE **ANSWERS**.

//////////// *I am determined,* ////////////

resilient and know I need to keep moving.

I AM ENTHUSIASTIC,

OPTIMISTIC
and energetic everyday

Conclusion

I had a hunch – a hunch that the 12 truths would get heads nodding. I spent 12 months asking if the 12 truths felt right, working through the pain points women experience, interviewing, questioning and challenging them.

In response to the 12 truths, I launched one of my programs, Thriving Women. I spent the year with a fantastic group of women across Melbourne and Perth – women from large organisations, women who have their own businesses, women who want more, women who know they have more to give and are unafraid to give it a crack. Go-getters, if you will.

The women I spoke to agreed that to move forward, you need to understand yourself, your strengths and how to leverage them, how to personally go about getting results, how to build your resilience and how to have the right network. They were prepared to reflect on the 12 truths and ask themselves, "Is this me? Is this something I am worried about? What can I do about it?"

Are you merely surviving in your career or business? Wouldn't you love to thrive?

Now is the time to focus on taking your leadership or business to the next level. It's time to step up, lean in and get shiz done. It's time to show the world your potential. It's no good if you are the world's best-kept secret. It's time to use your passion, align with your purpose and get paid what you are worth. It's time to be a go-getter.

We all have the same 24 hours, the same 86,400 seconds each day. How will you make your day count? What will you choose?

Go get it!

About the Author

I truly, wholeheartedly believe in the potential of women. I'm the mother of three daughters and I'm someone who is a proud member of the glass-half-full brigade. I can't possibly believe in any other alternative than women doing work they love. Each person has a glass that is always full of hopes, doubts, results, failures and successes, yet they love drinking their cocktail because they choose what goes in their glass. They are in control.

If the contents of your glass don't match your aspirations, then we need to design a better mix, full to the brim. Life is too short to drink the wrong cocktail!

The women I work with often surprise themselves more than they ever surprise me. You see, as an optimist, I have a knack for seeing possibilities everywhere, even when people can't see the opportunities themselves. Actually, it's more than a knack; I'm qualified and highly experienced in performance management and coaching.

I love working with women who are driven and passionate about their work, yet need some guidance to feel empowered. Coaching women to achieve incredible results is my professional and personal sweet spot because my work is fulfilling and plays to my strengths. My passion and purpose are aligned, and so Monday morning is something I embrace with excitement; hence, my tagline – be enthusiastic, optimistic and energetic every day!

Work With Me

The Thriving Women program is one way to work with me, but there are plenty of others. Here are a few:

- **One-on-one business coaching and mentoring**

  I work with a limited number of clients to help them take their business or teams to the next level. My work as a coach is focused on ensuring women have what they need to be fulfilled, excited and engaged with their working lives. Why? Because it has an indisputable flow-on effect to their broader lives. The goal of my coaching is for women, whatever their role, to feel energised by their work and clear about what success means to them. Our work together is based on practical, logical next steps to create momentum that leads to progress, and progress that leads to success, regardless of how it is defined.

- **Executive teams**

  I work closely with executive teams to give them the opportunity to have deeper conversations. I give them the space to reflect on who they are as leaders and where they are as a team, and how to work together more effectively.

- **Tailored leadership development programs**

  I run tailored leadership development programs for senior leaders within organisations, enabling them to step back from the day-to-day operations to focus on strategy and their people.

For more information about my programs:

- Go to www.emmamcqueen.com.au
- Email emma@emmamcqueen.com.au
- Phone +61419521946

Connect With Me

LinkedIn:
www.linkedin.com/in/emmamcqueen

Instagram:
www.instagram.com/emmarmcqueen/

Facebook:
www.facebook.com/emmarmcqueen/

References

1. "A statistical snapshot of women in the Australian workforce." Department of Employment, Skills, Small and Family Business. (2019). www.employment.gov.au/newsroom/statistical-snapshot-women-australian-workforce

2. "Australia's gender equality scorecard: Key fndings from the Workplace Gender Equality Agency's 2017–18 reporting data." Workplace Gender Equality Agency. (2018).

3. Kay, K. and Shipman, C. (2014). *The Confidence Code*. HarperCollins Publishers.

4. "Fixed mindset vs. growth mindset: What really matters for success." (2019). Develop Good Habits. www.developgoodhabits.com/fixed-mindset-vs-growth-mindset/

5. "Fixed mindset vs. growth mindset: What really matters for success." (2019). Develop Good Habits. www.developgoodhabits.com/fixed-mindset-vs-growth-mindset/

6. "Why do mindsets matter?" Mindset Works. www.mindsetworks.com/Science/Impact

7. Harter, J. (2018). "Dismal employee engagement is a sign of global mismanagement." Gallup. www.gallup.com/workplace/231668/dismal-employee-engagement-sign-global-mismanagement.aspx

8. Moola, N. (2019). "Confidence is like compound interest: In the short term it's hard to notice, in the long term, it's crucial." Daily Maverick. www.dailymaverick.co.za/opinionista/2019-10-10-confidence-is-like-compound-interest-in-the-short-term-its-hard-to-notice-in-the-long-term-its-crucial/

9. Half, R. (2018). "12 characteristics of an effective manager." Robert Half. www.roberthalf.com.au/blog/employers/12-characteristics-effective-manager

10. Trimboli, O. (2017). *Deep Listening: Impact Beyond Words.* www.oscartrimboli.com/wp-content/uploads/2017/12/Deep-Listening-Whitepaper_Oscar-Trimboli.pdf

11. Guillen, L. (2018). "Is the confidence gap between men and women a myth?" Harvard Business Review. hbr.org/2018/03/is-the-confidence-gap-between-men-and-women-a-myth

12. McDermott, E. (2016). "Women often undersell their experience and capabilities, while men don't think twice about it." The Journal.ie. www.thejournal.ie/readme/women-working-2642459-Mar2016/

13. Kay, K. and Shipman, C. (2014). *The Confidence Code.* HarperCollins Publishers.

14. Hollis, R. (2018). *Girl, Wash Your Face.* US: Thomas Nelson Publishers.

15. "What is happiness? Explained." Black Dog Institute. (2019). www.blackdoginstitute.org.au/news/news-detail/2019/03/18/what-is-happiness-explained

16. "What is happiness? Explained." Black Dog Institute. (2019). www.blackdoginstitute.org.au/news/news-detail/2019/03/18/what-is-happiness-explained

17. "Do more and have fun with time management." Francesco Cirillo. francescocirillo.com/pages/pomodoro-technique

18. organisecuratedesign.com/

19. nicolevine.com.au/

20. Reh, F.J. (2019). "In pursuit of work and life balance." The Balance Careers. www.thebalancecareers.com/work-life-balance-and-juggling-glass-and-rubber-balls-2275864

21. Harris, R. (2015). "The loneliness epidemic: We're more connected than ever – but are we feeling more alone?" Independent. www.independent.co.uk/life-style/health-and-families/features/the-loneliness-epidemic-more-connected-than-ever-but-feeling-more-alone-10143206.html

22. "Multitasking doesn't work: The realities and the research behind one of our favorite bad habits." reMarkable. (2018). blog.remarkable.com/multitasking-doesnt-work-the-realities-and-the-research-behind-one-of-our-favorite-bad-habits-60e2d6fe0e30

23. Etkin, J. and Mogilner, C. (2015). "When multitasking makes you happy and when it doesn't." Harvard Business Review. hbr.org/2015/02/when-multitasking-makes-you-happy-and-when-it-doesnt

24. Cherry, K. (2019). "How multitasking affects productivity and brain health." VeryWellMind. www.verywellmind.com/multitasking-2795003

25. Discovery in Action. discoveryinaction.com.au/

26. Martin, L., Ball, A. (2019). "Australia's gender pay gap still 14%, with men earning $240 more a week than women." The Guardian. www.theguardian.com/world/2019/aug/15/australias-gender-pay-gap-still-14-with-men-earning-240-more-a-week-than-women

27. You can also download the self-care plan template from here: gallery.mailchimp.com/895def69fe9850b8cb9dea9d6/files/77b4f9c5-544f-4e5d-b727-687eedf887e9/Self_Care_Plan.02.pdf

28. "Quiz: are you addicted to your smartphone?" Deakin University. this.deakin.edu.au/self-improvement/are-nuts-making-you-fat

29. "Fake it till you make it." Wikipedia. en.wikipedia.org/wiki/Fake_it_till_you_make_it

30. Holtzclaw, E. (2019). "Power of consistency: 5 rules." www.inc.com/eric-v-holtzclaw/consistency-power-success-rules.html

31. Dean, S. (2018). "Here's how long it really takes to break a habit, according to science." Science Alert. www.sciencealert.com/how-long-it-takes-to-break-a-habit-according-to-science

32. "Proof that you should get a life." The Economist. (2014). www.economist.com/free-exchange/2014/12/09/proof-that-you-should-get-a-life

33. www.jimcollins.com/

34. janinegarner.com.au/

35. janinegarner.com.au/books/